Praise for LIVE, LAUGH, LOVE AGAIN

"An extrordinarily honest look at the lives of four women going through divorce. One minute you'll be laughing, and the next you'll be in tears as you get to know these women on a personal level. An inspiring read on how each one survived her traumatic journey by embracing her faith and clinging to the *one* man who never left her side. A must-read for every woman contemplating or going through divorce."

—Kathy Troccoli, singer, speaker, and author

"This book is for every divorced woman who has believed her life is over, the tears will never end, and her heart will never feel again. Let these words of hope reach into your darkness and lift you up with their truth. Our great God still has an amazing life full of love and laughter waiting for you."

—Angela Thomas, bestselling author of *Do You Think I'm Beautiful?*

Live, Laugh, Love Again

A Christian Woman's Guide to Surviving Divorce

MICHELLE BORQUEZ,

CONNIE WETZELL,

ROSALIND SPINKS-SEAY, AND

CARLA SUE NELSON

WARNER
Faith

New York Boston Nashville

Warner Faith

Time Warner Book Group

1271 Avenue of the Americas, New York, NY 10020

The Warner Faith name and logo are registered trademarks of the
Time Warner Book Group.

Printed in the United States

Illustrations by Trish Cramblet

ISBN: 0-7394-6916-9

ISBN 13: 978-0-7394-6916-3

To the hurting women who think all hope is lost, the counselors who help us want to live, the friends and children who make us laugh, and our heavenly Father, who never leaves us and who lovingly shows us that we can still feel love.

Contents

Contents

Foreword

by Dr. Tim Clinton

Unfortunately, divorce happens, and Christians are far from exempt. A recent study by The Barna Group shows that rates of divorce among Christians are identical to those of the non-Christian population ("Born Again Christians Just as Likely to Divorce as Non-Christians," September 8, 2004). Moreover, data shows that such divorces occur *after* the married persons have accepted Christ as their Savior. In fact, multiple divorces are extraordinarily common among born-again Christians: 23 percent are divorced two or more times!

I am not an advocate of divorce, and I very rarely if ever counsel for the dissolution of marriage. Many women, however, face situations with no other option—and they have little or no help from family, friends, or the church, That is why I am pleased to have a resource such as *Live, Love, Laugh Again*.

The open dialogue this book provides shows women that they are not alone in their experiences. Readers journey with the authors through their stories, learn the dynamics and processes of a troubled marriage, and examine the heartbreaking aspects of a marital split. In addition, readers will benefit from sections such as "Fruitful Steps," "Life Lessons," and the "Survival Checklist." And all of this is delivered in a way that is sincere, gripping, and surprisingly funny!

I believe God journeys with those who travel. He says to us, "Never will I leave you; never will I forsake you" (Heb. 13:5 NIV), and we know that "neither height nor depth, nor anything else in all creation, will be able to separate us from the love of God that is Christ Jesus our Lord" (Rom. 8:39 NIV).

The reward for those who diligently seek Him is strength for the journey. Any woman who turns to our compassionate, merciful, and forgiving Savior in her time of need will find that He guides her steps and helps her to live, love, and laugh again.

Preface

Preface, disclaimer, whatever you want to call it—this is the part of the book where we want to emphasize that this is not a male-bashing book. We repeat: *This is not a male-bashing book.* You must read the entire book to see our stories come full circle and gauge the full compass of grief as it turns to joy, because each chapter reflects a different stage in the grieving and healing process. We all admit that it takes "two to tango," as they say, and we know we each played a part in the end of our marriages. If some of the stories seem skewed to make us look better than our former spouses, it is not intentional. It is simply our way of recalling the past through the only eyes we have—our own. The purpose of this book is not to belittle, slander, insult, malign, libel, smear, disparage, vilify, defame, defile, or maim our ex-spouses or anyone else. We would love to read a book on this subject written by our former husbands and hear their "Mars" side of the story. It would be fascinating. To them, we say, "Go for it."

It is also absolutely not our intention to make light of the institution of marriage. In fact, if you are contemplating divorce and hoping this book will help you "get the upper hand"—*stop*! Do not pass "Go." Do not collect $200! Instead, go grab your honey, give him a big, wet kiss and drag him to the counselor's office. Fake it until you make it! Here's a paraphrase of Malachi 2:16: *God hates divorce!* God can restore *anything*.

However, if your spouse has already divorced you emotionally or legally, by all means, grab your box of tissues and read on.

This is not a book about revenge or a woman's scorn. It is not about money (although some of us are still paying off legal bills and credit cards from "shopping therapy," so we recommend you buy several copies for friends, family, and church libraries!). In all seriousness, it is not our intention to hurt but to heal. Writing is therapeutic, and in pouring out our feelings onto paper, we have sealed up some of the cracks in our hearts. Women are communicators, pure and simple. We are story tellers, and we benefit from hearing

other women's stories. Why do you think soaps, Lifetime®
TV, and talk shows are predominantly viewed by women?
Look at Oprah's success. We love her; she is the queen of
"the story."

As Christian women, it is important that we openly discuss this issue and share our stories. Only in recent years
have churches allowed support groups and classes like Divorce Care™ and acknowledged this epidemic that is destroying their congregations. There are now accountability
groups for men and women and even "Blended Family"
Sunday School classes. Churches are also trying to prevent
this plague with retreats, conferences, and premarital counseling.

We want to add our voices to the growing number of resources that hurting women need to help them heal. To reassure them—you—that they are not alone, because life can
be extremely tough. When you think you've reached the
bottom, you've got to roll with the punches and trust God
for everything. That's what this book is all about. As popu-
lar speaker and Christian author Thelma Wells so eloquently quotes from the Bible, *"Be anxious for no-thang!"*
Amen, sisters! Let the healing begin!

Introduction

If you are reading this book, then you most likely have already faced the initial shock of approaching, going through, or trying to get over a divorce. You are not alone. About half of all marriages end in divorce, according to *Divorce for Dummies* by John Ventura and Mary Reed (and probably any other book on the subject that you have picked up or that a well-meaning friend has given you).[1] However, this book isn't about statistics and psychology—we leave that to the experts. Instead, we want to help you understand all of the feelings you are having, have had, and will have. And we want you to know that, girlfriend, we have been there and done that!

So . . . how did this book come about? Well, how do most things happen with women? Lisa calls Jackie, Jackie calls Tammy, Tammy calls you. Either you have some great idea you are all conjuring up, or disaster has hit the friendships due to a major miscommunication, and you are then forced to spend hours on the phone trying to put the relationships back on firm footing.

For Carla, Connie, Roz, and me (Michelle), it was the "great idea" scenario. Connie, who we call "The Conz," called me up one afternoon and began to share with me the journey she had been on since her divorce. As she opened up her heart and gave the details of her life, I began to realize how much I resonated with her story from the pain in my own life. Immediately, a bond, a friendship of communal experience developed.

From the time I found out my husband wanted a divorce until the divorce was actually final, I felt completely alone. No one understood the tremendous pain, rejection, and devastation I felt. No one understood the great loss I had suffered. No one understood the feelings of anger and depression, even the continuous thoughts of suicide that had run through my mind . . . until now. Now, here was this woman who not only understood me, but also had actually experienced the same things I had. I ended our phone call feeling greatly affirmed by our conversation.

Then I began to wonder: *Why couldn't someone have been*

there during *my divorce?* If only I had had a friend who understood my pain and loss during that time—someone who didn't think divorce was a disease she and her husband could catch, someone who didn't always point out my faults, even if she did mean well.

My next thought after hanging up with Connie was: *Our connection made me feel so much better. How can we help other women know they are not alone?* As a writer and editor of a magazine for women, my focus and passion in recent years has been to make a positive difference and bring life-changing, valuable tools to women. I realized I wanted to help women going through divorce know—in a way I never did—they are not alone.

I later called Connie again, and we immediately began to discuss ways we could offer help to women facing the same crisis we had recently faced ourselves. Within a week we called Carla and Roz, our mutual friends and fellow comrades, and asked them to come on board with this venture. They, too, shared our excitement and passion to help women through their experience of divorce. Thus, the team—and this book—was born. We are the Fearsome Four! Four women from different walks of life, at different ages in life, and in different stages of life who are on a mission to help women who find themselves in the throes of a divorce or who are still recovering from the aftermath. Each one of us can identify with your pain. We can identify with your loss, and we can definitely identify with your divorce. Each one of us has been there. We can all testify to feeling like Humpty Dumpty, who fell off the wall and broke into a million pieces. We have all been through the process of being put back together again, and we now have a passion to take the remnants of our brokenness and watch the Lord recreate something of value with them. We want women everywhere to overcome as we have overcome.

Through the experience of this book, we have not only become great friends, but also we have become each other's cheerleaders. We have prayed, cried, and grown to love one another. Now we want to cheer you on while you walk through your own painful journey back to abundant life.

To give you a better picture of us, I (Michelle) will introduce you to my coauthors:

Carla has the brilliant sense of humor. She has made us laugh many a night. This Georgia peach, originally from Atlanta, has a smile that is contagious, and her laugh is just as catching! I remember the first day we met. I had not even planned to mention to her that I was divorced. Our meeting was strictly business, and I was going to keep it that way. I don't know how we got on the topic, but suddenly I found myself listening to her incredible story of how God had redeemed her circumstances after divorce. My divorce was still fresh and I was still recovering, so it was encouraging to meet another woman who had gone through such similar circumstances and see her sitting in front of me doing great! She openly shared her heart with me, and I opened my heart to her. I was so relieved to find out the emotions

I experienced had been normal. I thought I was the only one who had felt and reacted the way I did.

Looking back, I see what a big step it must have been for Carla to allow herself to be vulnerable and open up to me, a complete stranger. Compassion is definitely one of her gifts. She is so determined to use the gifts God has given her to help women in their crises. Besides being the mother of three adorable children, she is a marketing and public relations professional who trusts this book will impact the lives of millions and that her personal journey will encourage women everywhere to have hope for tomorrow. Some see the glass half full and others see it half empty; Carla is just happy to have the glass.

Rosalind is our hero and is affectionately known to us as "Roz." She is absolutely amazing—a reserved intellectual with a shining light in her eyes that reveals her love for our Lord. We all admire her for her tremendous courage, discipline, and strength. She is a single mom with one son who is the light of her life. As we were writing the book Roz was working full time and putting herself through graduate school for a master's degree in psychology.

Somehow this compassionate lady also finds a way to serve as a facilitator with Divorce Care, a divorce recovery group she has been involved with for the five years since her divorce. Roz plans to use her knowledge and experience to counsel other women who have gone through the devastation of divorce. She is passionate about her relationship with Christ and would give her last breath to share the

Live, Laugh, Love Again

Good News. She is committed to waiting on God's plan when it comes to getting remarried. (However, we—her three coauthors—are determined to have her "fixed up" by the time you read these words in print!)

Connie "The Conz" is the typical passionate Italian woman. Think Rocky Balboa in the form of a beautiful, petite brunette with a great sense of humor. Just being around her cracks us up. (Between The Conz and Carla, Roz and I usually spend our time trying not to roll on the floor in out-of-control hysterics.) The Conz can be quite the character, but when it comes down to it she is solid as a rock. I find her desire to know more of God so very genuine. I think God looks down at Connie and laughs and cries at the same time. Laughs because He can't help but chuckle at most of the things she says, and cries because He is so pleased with the ultimate position of her heart! She has been such a joy to get to know.

Connie has a passion and complete dedication to contribute to the lives of those who are broken. Originally from Chicago, she is a multitalented woman who has worked in radio and as voice talent for various recordings of Scripture readings. She is the dedicated mom of two gorgeous grown daughters. When she's not working on another radio or print project, you will find her in a yoga class or in her kitchen making the most amazing "red sauce" you have ever tasted.

Now it's time for the rest of us to tell you about Michelle. Affectionately known as "Media Superwoman," Michelle is the proud mother of six children (four biologically) as well as a former model, radio host, respected author, and founder and editor-in-chief of *Shine* magazine. This proud Texan is as much at home making Breakfast Quesadillas with Jalapeño Tortillas for her amazing husband and children as she is chatting with First Lady Laura Bush for a cover story for the magazine.

Michelle is one of those women who can juggle a hundred things at once and not let anything drop. Plus, she has amazing skin that we all envy. Her positive attitude is what makes everything work. She will tackle anything, and she really does think that *all* things are possible. It's good to surround yourself with people like Michelle, especially when you're going through a tough situation like divorce. Michelle's heart for the Lord and her belief that God can heal all drives her as she seeks out every opportunity to help women, even if it means "spilling her guts" and using her own personal story.

Altogether, we are four completely different women from completely different backgrounds. We each have our own unique story, but as we wrote this book, we found amazing similarities in the ways we worked through divorce and ultimately got past it. We say this to remind you that you are in a lot of good company when it comes to your hurt, your grief, your anger, your humiliation, and ultimately, we pray, your complete healing and restoration. Divorce knows no boundaries. It comes to every race, socio-economic class, education level, and faith. Christians are certainly no exception.

But regardless of how we all got to that painful place, we—Michelle, Carla, Connie, and Rosalind—are living proof that you will survive the "death" of divorce with the help of the one true God who will never leave you. You can do it! We know, because we did. And we want to help you through it, too. While we cannot be with you physically to hold you in your pain, to cry with you in your loss, to ache with you when you are alone, we can share with you in the pages of this book our pain, our loss, and, most important, our paths to recovery.

In each chapter, you will hear some of our stories, as we share what we experienced. We'll walk you through the stages of grief that accompany divorce—shock, denial, anger, depression and, finally, acceptance, and healing. We'll give you some personal pointers and end each chapter with our Final Thoughts and some of the Life Lessons learned along the way. Finally, we will give you Five Fruitful Steps (action points to get you started on your road to recovery) and Survival Checklists, as well as resources and Scriptures to point you in your new direction. We hope these tools will help you experience God's hand at work in your lives as never before.

Most of all, we hope that this book will serve as a reminder that you are never alone. Not only are there plenty of women out there, like us, who know what you're going through and who care deeply, but also there is a God who plans to "prosper you and not to harm you," who loves you so much that He has special plans to "give you hope and a future" (Jer. 29:11 NIV). That may be hard to believe right now, but it's a promise! Isn't that awesome?

So relax, read on, and remember your journey to recovery begins with the understanding that . . .

You will live,
You will laugh,
And, yes, you will love again!

Live, Laugh,
Love Again

Chapter 1

Facing the Unthinkable–Shock

"For with God nothing will be impossible."
—*Luke 1:37 NKJV*

F eel like you just got run over by that train? That chug-a-chug-a-choo-choo steam engine of D-I-V-O-R-C-E that hits you hard right in the chest, then finishes the job by nailing your caboose? We—Michelle, Rosalind, Connie, and Carla—have all been stranded on those tracks, and we want to start by sharing our stories with you. Through our stories, we learn from each other—to live, laugh, and love again!

Women, by nature, are the story tellers, the collectors and keepers of memories (good and bad!) and traditions. We women are the ones who scrapbook (or at least collect the supplies to do it someday). We are the ones who write the Christmas newsletters every year. And we are the ones who hang little Olivia's latest artistic rendering on the fridge. We want to show the world our story (and it doesn't hurt that Olivia's stick-figure rendering of Mommy is oh-so-flattering: always skinny and with hair that's truly blonde).

What we're saying is that women live and breathe the details of life. Think about the difference in the way men and women give directions. Men tell you about north and south and rattle off street names and mileage estimations. The only landmark they might note is a speed trap any-where along the way.

For example, a man would say: Take I-65 North, exit Veteran's Parkway to Centerpoint. Go left for approximately 8.6 miles. Be sure to really stop before turning; there's a motorcycle cop hiding out. Turn southeast onto Bonita Parkway, and you're there.

We women tell the story: Okay, you know the road that Sam's Club and Target are on, right? Take that and go through lots of red lights toward Gallatin. Pass McDonald's on your right, and keep going past the park where the boys play ball. After you pass Wal-Mart, turn right, and you're there. If you go past the cute little consignment store with the really good stuff (which has an extra 25 percent-off sale going on right now) and the YMCA, then you've gone too far. Oh, and speaking of discounts, did I tell you Jackie can get you an extra 15 percent off at Ann Taylor? Yes, an extra discount on top of the clearance price, *yada, yada, yada* . . .

You get the point.

Our stories are like landmarks that highlight our journey through life. When you hit a rough crossing, it's nice to look up and see signs that remind you you're not the only one to have come this way. It is comforting to know others have traveled across these same hills and valleys and have returned to tell about them.

The freight train of divorce may have already hit you full force, and you're busy pulling the pieces of your life up off the tracks. Perhaps you have already made progress on this journey, coming to the realization that divorce sucks (You go, girl—acceptance is good!) but that it's survivable. Or perhaps you are caught under the weight of the train this very moment, or feel it barreling down upon you, and you know there is nothing you can do to stop it. You are crying from the pit of your stomach and don't even recognize the sounds coming from your throat. You are empty inside . . . utterly hollow. You feel terminally ill, as if you are dying.

You will get through it. The feelings are sheer agony, but you will crawl out from under that train. You might feel as though you're in pieces, because half of you has been ripped away. That's okay. Even if you are the one driving the Divorce Train, the actual process at some point will feel a little like open-heart surgery without anesthesia. For when marriage occurs, the Bible says that the two people become "one." And you can't split "one" without spilling blood on the tracks. But you can and will keep moving forward. At some point you will face the shock that life as you knew it is over and begin to realize that now you must find a way to regroup and move on. Here's how it began for us:

Carla

"Happy Mother's Day!"

That's right, for me it was Mother's Day, two weeks before our ninth wedding anniversary, when I first heard the words, "It's over." I had packed my best nightie and flown up to where my pilot husband was to "surprise" him. (Guess who got the surprise?) I knew my marriage was on rocky ground, and I wasn't really happy after being together for fifteen years. (We dated for six years before our marriage.) But I had no idea how unhappy he was.

I had come from Nashville to Chicago just to spend the night with him during his layover between flights. The airport was nearly empty, and it was very late. I had been waiting for hours, but it didn't matter because I was really thrilled about surprising him. As he walked up the Jetway and I saw him standing there in his flight uniform, it took my breath away. It was the same feeling I'd had the first time I caught sight of him when he was sixteen years old and stood at attention in his Air Force uniform at a Civil Air Patrol meeting. My mind whirred as I acknowledged this weekend was exactly what we needed to rekindle those feelings we'd first had for each other so long ago.

My sappy dream state quickly snapped back to reality as

I realized my hubby was not exactly thrilled to see me. How did I know this? Well, the reception was not exactly warm. He hesitantly walked over to me and, in an annoyed tone, asked why I was there as he quickly ushered me down the terminal and away from his coworkers. Then he abruptly said he'd left his cell phone on the plane. I stood there giddy and smiling like a complete idiot while he went back, supposedly to retrieve it. I just didn't get it. I had a romantic evening on my mind. He definitely did not.

We walked from the airport to his crash pad. A crash pad, for those of you not familiar with airline pilot lingo, is a house or apartment pilots share in the city they are based in so they have a "home away from home," a place to "crash" after a tough day of flying. It was not humorous at the time, but now I can laugh as I think of how ironic it was that the "crash pad" would be exactly the place where our marriage "crashed." (Hint: You can laugh at this, too, and at anything else you can. It will help balance all the tears.) I couldn't put my finger on it, but he was definitely acting very strangely. He had been this way for months, but I just thought it was the pressure of training and starting his big new job with the airlines.

You could cut the tension with a knife as we sat down in the living room of the thankfully empty house. He picked a single chair, and I lounged on the sofa, wondering all the while why he was not joining me. I knew I looked okay. I had recently lost nearly fifty pounds (pounds I had put on in the process of having our daughter and son) by working out at the gym, push-mowing part of our five-acre farm, and barely eating. I knew we'd had a tough couple of years with new babies, building a house, and job changes. So I was now very anxious to start our evening of romance in my new skin. The thought never entered my mind that I was going to hear the words "It's over" come out of his mouth.

But that's what he said. He was not a "talker," and that night was no exception. He just sat there and said, "It's over." For a moment I didn't even understand. Then it hit me that he meant our marriage. With those two little words, I felt like my heart had been carved out of my chest. I couldn't breathe; I felt sucker-punched.

At a moment like that, a thousand things go through your mind: *Is he gay? Cheating? What is wrong with me? Surely, we can find a way to work it out?* When I asked him why, his answer was simply that he didn't love me anymore and that he wasn't sure if he had ever loved me. *Wham!* Another one to the gut.

I didn't think I could hurt any worse. I was obviously mistaken! A blurry memory of a white dress and glowing candles in a little church flashed into my mind. Then the tears started as I thought about our history and all that we had built together—a home, children, dreams, sacrifices I'd made for him. Now he was calmly saying it was all for naught? I sat horrified at the thought that my babies were not conceived in love.

Despite our rocky times, I had never doubted I loved him. And I'd never thought I would be hearing otherwise from the man I had built my life around. Everything I was, my very identity, was wrapped up in him and his flying. Our wedding cake had said "Copilots for life" on it, for heaven's sake! One of our baby announcements claimed that our "aircraft company" had released a "new model with a wingspan of 19½ inches and a gross landing weight of 8 pounds, 3 ounces, with full-screaming throttle." Now all of that was suddenly gone.

No matter how long you have been married, divorce is the death of a covenant, a dream, your family. It is the end of a season of your life. It can feel like the end of your whole life. I begged and pleaded and asked my husband why. He said the news shouldn't come as a shock since he knew I was unhappy, too. I thought about that. About how frustrating it had been to see that even when he was home from trips, he didn't seem thrilled to be there and was often on the computer or talking on his cell phone in the backyard. I remembered all of the fights over the previous year and the horrid things I had said trying to "shock" him into wanting to be with me and the children instead of taking on extra flights. I had even used the "D" word (Divorce) myself in describing how miserable I was and how lonely I felt.

I guess he couldn't take the hysterics and begging, because he retreated to one of the bedrooms. Frantically I tried to get a grip. I slipped into my nightie and did the best I could—with puffy eyes and post-nasal drip from uncontrollable crying—to seduce him, thinking that would make everything all right. He turned away from me as he had in

CARLA'S LIFE LESSONS
The Shock Stage

When you are delivered a wounding blow like the words, "I want a divorce," your first reaction may be to curl up and die, to wander around in a daze, or to just sit and wallow. It's okay to do any or all of those things—in fact, it's normal during the shock stage.

The trick is to get up and go on. Work on turning your focus outward. Keep a schedule and routine so that your shock and grief don't become isolating and overwhelming. Consciously make that effort, as impossible as it may seem, so that you can eventually concentrate on the important things you'll need to do.

the past, especially in the last few months. I sat there in the dark, alone, crying myself to sleep, and thinking of my shattered marriage and my precious babies at home. They were just two and four, and I knew this "crash" would affect them for the rest of their lives. Happy Mother's Day to me!

As I boarded the earliest flight out of Midway Airport the next morning, I absolutely could not stop crying. I was completely numb, and the tears just kept falling. I barely recall my husband making a half-hearted attempt to board the plane. The flight attendant must have felt sorry for me when she saw that I wasn't even paying attention to my running nose, because she provided some tissues.

I was lost in my memories. I remembered the vacation we had taken with my husband's parents a few months earlier. I had felt like I was in Las Vegas with a stranger; it was obvious he was uncomfortable even then. While his mom and dad were out grooving to Wayne Newton, I had thought we might stay in and do some "grooving" of our own in the privacy of our own room. Let's just say that didn't happen. He left the hotel room to get ice so many times I though he might be trying to build an igloo in the desert.

You would think this would have been a red flag to me, but it wasn't. And it was pretty much the same at home. Now it was clear to me my luck would not change, even in Vegas. I thought of how he didn't even want his picture taken with me at Hoover Dam when his parents offered. Sitting there on the plane, crying my eyes out and thinking of all this, I started to wonder how long he had been planning to tell me.

Then my thoughts turned again to our sweet babies at home: *How on earth could he do this to them?* Their innocence would be lost forever.

I had a car at the Nashville Airport but could barely walk, much less drive. Thank the Lord for my sweet angel friend Melissa. She left work and picked me up as I tried to figure out how I would ever be able to pick up the pieces of my life.

Connie

"Fred Finds Wilma"

For me, it was Father's Day (What is it with holidays?), a day that started out beautifully and ended up as the worst day of my life to this point. I was left with a bullet that landed in my heart and created a hole that can never be filled again. The bleeding has finally stopped, but the hole is still there. (At this point you may be thinking, *This chick watches way too many "Mafia" flicks*, but this is the truth as I remember it.)

I was driving home after spending a week away, taking our older daughter to do her internship. The drive home was lovely. The sun was shining brightly, and I was eagerly looking forward to seeing my husband. He had called me several times during that week, and we'd had good conversations, all ending with "I love you." When I got home, as I was putting things away and going through the mail, I noticed that he seemed particularly quiet and deep in thought. He was watching some sporting event on TV but didn't seem very interested in what was going on. He was distracted.

I felt bad because it was Father's Day and I had wanted to cook him a special meal, but I arrived home late in the afternoon. So I told him I'd take him to dinner at the restaurant of his choice. After dinner, I suggested we go have coffee. He said he didn't feel like it. I immediately knew something was really wrong because he *always* wants coffee. I asked him what was going on, and he said we needed to talk. (Hint: This was a red flag! Most men do not enjoy talking!)

My heart sank. He'd had a physical three days earlier. I thought he was going to tell me he was sick with some terminal disease. No, I'm not just being a dramatic Italian. What he told me was actually worse. I never could have conjured this one up, even in my over-imaginative mind.

What he said still seems so surreal. We sat in the car, and

he proceeded to tell me of an old high-school sweetheart he'd been e-mailing for the past three months. While I was away, he went to see her. During the one week that I was gone, he decided that he no longer loved me but instead was in love with her. He also told me that he had been unhappy with me for the last ten years or so, that he was planning on leaving me anyway, and that now was a good time because our kids were grown up and we wouldn't have to deal with custody issues.

I was shocked at this admission because I'd never known he was unhappy and literally had not seen any signs to prove it. I was also confused, because just three short weeks before, he had taken me on a romantic weekend getaway to a bed and breakfast where we discussed our five-year plans and dreams. In short, until that moment, if I'd had one million dollars, I would have bet every last dime of it on the security of my marriage. I say that just to give you an idea of how shocked I was when he laid this on me. I totally did not see it coming!

Now I heard the scream of the whistle as the high-speed train hit me. Then my mind tried to reason it away: *This won't last. This is just a phase—a midlife crisis. We can fix this. He's just gone temporarily insane. After all, we have been married for twenty-six years. We can't just throw that away.*

It was so not fair! Our two girls were grown, and the younger one was just getting ready to move out. It was finally going to be our time to be alone and rekindle our flame. Well, he was rekindling, just not with me!

He said it was only our musical backgrounds that brought us together. That we were too young when we married. That we got married for the wrong reasons. And that after all these years, we'd grown apart. (Sometimes, I think there's a book out there called *How to Dump Your Spouse* because it seems as though the lines are always the same, doesn't it?)

He told me about conversations we'd had in the past that I did not remember the way he did. They were completely different. It made me think I was going crazy. This, I find, is a common factor with couples that are having problems. I really believe they play out a conversation in their minds and then believe they verbalized words that in reality they only thought. I could particularly see this happening in my husband's case because he was not a communicator. He didn't like to confront. He believed issues of conflict would resolve themselves over time.

I begged for a three- to six-month run with a counselor before throwing in the towel on our twenty-six-year marriage. He declined, saying counseling doesn't work. My daughter made an emergency trip back from where I had just taken her for her internship. Both my girls ordered a family meeting, as they were both devastated after hearing this news from their dad. They cried like never before, begging their dad to try to work things out. I'll never forget what he told them that night as they sat there with tears streaming down their faces. He said, "I can either stay and make the three of you happy, or I can leave and make myself happy; and I choose to leave."

When he made up his mind, there was no reasoning with him. He told me he was leaving for a month to think and pray about the situation. I was encouraged, but I begged him to not have any contact with *her* for that month because his thoughts would be cluttered and distorted and he wouldn't be able to hear what God was saying. He said he wasn't sure he could do that.

Over the next few days, I felt so desperate. I took a long, hard look at myself and asked for his forgiveness and just one chance to make things right. I repented, groveled, and begged my husband not to leave. I assumed all of the responsibility for our marriage failing. I told him I'd go anywhere and do anything it took to salvage our relationship. He assured me that he had not been physically intimate with the other woman (Sound familiar, anyone?) but that he loved her, not me, and that was that.

According to him, there was no hope. It was over.

I can honestly say that when divorce occurs against your will, it feels worse than death. I really think it would have been easier on me if he had died. With natural death, even-

CONNIE'S LIFE LESSONS
The Shock Stage

I think it is so important at first to grasp hold of your feelings and live in that painful moment. You won't stay there forever, but ignoring your feelings, hiding them, or "stuffing" them definitely won't make them go away. I get so perturbed when I hear people say, "I don't have a right to feel so bad when other people have it so much worse." Bull. Sorry, but can we be real here for a moment? No one knows how you feel, so let yourself experience the pain. If you don't, trust me, it's going to come out at some point.

tually there is closure. No one chooses to die. But in divorce, leaving is a choice.

After my begging for a week, he decided he was moving out anyway. The night he left, my younger daughter taught him how to do a load of laundry. He had never washed one load of clothes in twenty-six years.

Afterward, I sat in one of the corners of my home, which now felt too large, and sobbed like a baby. I was trying to come to terms with what was happening, but I was on an emotional roller coaster that was out of control. Within one week my life had taken a drastic turn. *Everything* was changing. For the first time in my entire life, I was alone. My husband was gone. My children were gone. I had to figure out how I could possibly survive without him.

Rosalind

"Alone Time with God?"

It was the weekend of Valentine's Day. We sat in a cozy, romantic restaurant, having a wonderful evening together, laughing and talking without any interruptions. We didn't talk about the baby or problems from work and ministry. Nor did we have any disagreements or arguments. It was a fun time—just the two of us.

We sat talking about our future together, and our past. We couldn't believe we had just celebrated three years of marriage last December. We'd had stress and tension in the relationship. We had a toddler who took up a lot of my time. I was operating an in-home daycare five days a week and sometimes during the evening. My husband was a graduate student working a full-time job and also serving as ministry leader at our church. There was no balance for all the activity going on in our lives, which affected our marriage. So this alone time together was something we both needed and wanted.

At least I did. Sitting there that night with my husband, divorce never entered my mind. I thought we were both on the same page, headed in the same direction. We'd vowed in December that we were committed to the marriage and were determined to make it work despite everything going on in our lives, and we were reaffirming that commitment that night.

Cut to the weekend *after* Valentine's Day. My dear, sweet husband encouraged me to go on a little getaway trip with my son to visit family so he could enjoy some "alone" time with God. Why would I think twice about it? I respected his desire. My husband spending time with God would only benefit our marriage and give him some time to really seek the purposes God had for him. Plus, spending time with family was always positive.

Looking back, I did think it a bit odd when I called him that Friday night and he didn't call me back. This probably should have been a red flag, but who knew? I dismissed it and assumed he was enjoying his special time with God so much that he forgot to call. I didn't call him again the whole weekend so as not to interrupt any prayer time he might have been having.

When I walked in the door that Sunday evening, he was there to welcome me with such a sweet smile. He asked me how my weekend had been, and I shared briefly how wonderful it had been to spend time with my family. Then he suddenly became serious and told me he needed to talk. Something in his tone, something in the way he said those words, made me respond with hesitation. I wondered what he wanted to discuss.

He began telling me how much he had enjoyed his time with God and how wonderful it was to get away. Then the conversation suddenly took a turn for the worse. He said (and sisters, can you believe this one?) God had "revealed" to him that our marriage was over. He told me God was releasing him from the marriage.

I felt numb. My mind simply couldn't compute what he was saying: *What? What in the world is he talking about?* I immediately ran away to our bedroom, got on my knees before God, and cried out to Him, asking if He had indeed revealed such a thing to my husband. In my heart, I knew that this was not of God—that there must be someone else.

To say that I was "surprised" is quite the understatement. Even "absolutely floored" doesn't cut it. There is no word in the English language that could describe how I felt. I couldn't sleep that night. I tossed and turned in a state of shock. "My husband is leaving me . . . My husband is leaving me . . ." ran through my mind over and over. I knew I had to get some rest because I had my babies from the day-care coming in the morning. So I tried to sleep.

But I couldn't. All I could think was, *How could this be happening to me?* I thought I had done everything I could to be a good wife and make a good life for my family. I had supported my husband in his schooling and his ministry and tried to love him with all of my heart. Yet now he was destroying all that we had built together.

The next day my husband stayed home from work. We tried to talk, but I was too numb to hear what he had to say. All day long, I was in shock. I couldn't even function in my job as caretaker at the daycare. All I could think was, *How am I going to tell the parents that my husband is leaving me and I have to close the daycare for good?*

I asked my husband if we could go to counseling. He told me he would go; however, he did not want to hear what the counselor had to say because he had already gotten his "Word from the Lord."

God gives you what you need when you least expect it. Two days later I was taking the trash out. When I opened the lid to the trash can, I noticed some bank statements inside. I took them out and looked to see who they belonged to, because I knew we didn't belong to the bank listed on the envelope. Well, you can guess what I saw—the statements belonged to my husband . . . with a different address. I couldn't believe it; he'd opened another account without letting me know.

I began to look at the statements and noticed a floral shop

ROSALIND'S LIFE LESSONS
The Shock Stage

Sisters, if you are in this stage, you probably feel like you're in a state of shock, especially if you weren't expecting your husband to leave you. Yes, it's painful right now and your world is probably upside down. So ask your friends and family to embrace you and bolster you. It is okay to scream at the top of your lungs or cry your eyes out. You are experiencing a loss that is devastating. God hears your cry and He knows your pain. Release yourself to Him and let Him comfort you and help you through this difficult time. Don't give up.

transaction on one of them—for Valentine's Day. I contacted the shop, explained to the lady that I was double-checking my statement and didn't recognize the transaction, and asked to whom the flowers had been sent.

She looked up the information. It wasn't good news. The flowers had been sent to another woman—someone I knew from church.

Now I was angry. I immediately contacted my husband, who tried to deny it, regardless of the proof. He tried to make excuses, explaining he'd had them sent from the church when her grandmother died. Which didn't explain the separate account. Or why he'd never mentioned it.

Of course there was no way, considering the circumstances, that we would end up doing anything other than arguing over the phone. I ended up hanging up on him. I was in so much pain. It was then that I truly began to realize I was losing my husband and there was nothing—I mean *nothing*—I could do to gain him back.

Michelle

"Midlife Crisis or Marriage Crisis?"

Unlike Carla, The Conz, and Roz, I knew long before the words "I want a divorce" were spoken that I was on a journey headed for disaster. I remember as vividly as if it was yesterday pleading with my husband, telling him where we were heading in the hopes that he would see it and agree we needed to be in counseling together. We had gone through a lot together in the thirteen years of our marriage. He had endured some personal and professional frustrations, but I always thought they were things we would get through. I kept thinking he was in some kind of midlife crisis and would recover. I had not "felt" love for him in quite some time, but I was raised to believe that love is commitment, even when feelings come and go, and that feelings can't always be trusted.

Still, it became very apparent that if something didn't change, my marriage would end as a train wreck. As each day passed, it felt as if my dream of the happily-ever-after marriage went with it. It was all slipping away, and my overwhelming feelings of helplessness were unbearable. I kept thinking to myself, *This can't be happening. This cannot be happening to me. This wasn't part of my plan. I am one of those "Till death do us part" kind of gals. What happened to our vows? What happened to the words "to hell and back"?* (Okay, the wedding vows don't actually say "to hell and back," but we all know that's what they mean.)

On the other hand, I have always been an eternal optimist (or maybe the eternal ostrich), so even though I thought I knew where our marriage was headed, the shock of actually arriving there was unbearably difficult to handle. I found myself wanting to run—although I had actually been "running," or at least avoiding, for at least a year before my divorce, to the extent that I had tried not to even be in the same room as my husband! I kept thinking somehow the problem would go away. Somehow it would all disappear. I thought wrong. This Cinderella was losing her prince and somehow couldn't fathom it.

Once upon a time when we were dating, my soon-to-be husband whispered to me in the middle of an incredibly romantic date, "Michelle, I want to take care of you for the rest of your life." I melted when I heard that—what woman wouldn't? Did I believe him when he said it? You bet I believed him. Now, almost fifteen years later, the words "I want a divorce" were being nicely delivered to me while on family vacation in Colorado. I knew before the trip that he was going to walk away, but it was my last attempt—a dream vacation that would somehow make everything better.

It was so surreal, almost like watching a version of the movie of my life. I felt as if someone else had taken over my body because I could no longer feel my fingers or toes. I quietly asked him, "Why? Why is this the end of everything we have worked so hard to build?"

The only answer he could give me was simply, "I just haven't painted on the tapestry of my life, and you have."

I couldn't believe my ears! Talk about shock! I don't know what was worse for me: his desire for a divorce or his lack of passion to try and save our marriage. Was I not worth even that? But he had made his decision long before he shared it with me, and there was nothing that would change his mind. He had already discussed everything with his lawyer and had begun the divorce proceedings before he even told me.

After he said he wanted a divorce, he shared that he had been unhappy for thirteen years and that he had never had the

MICHELLE'S LIFE LESSONS
The Shock Stage

Your feelings are very real, and it is important to be able to express them in a real way. It is not a time to tell yourself you are a Christian and therefore you shouldn't be feeling this way. In their book A Woman's Forbidden Emotion, authors H. Norman Wright and Dr. Gary J. Oliver state that "anger within a woman that goes unrecognized, unadmitted, and untouched becomes an unwanted resident that soon affects the totality of her life." Girls, recognize the situation and realize it is okay if you are angry. Just don't stay there!

same vision I did for our lives. I think the hardest thing for me to swallow was the news that he had been secretly planning our divorce *for two years!* I was truly devastated to hear that while I had been racking my brain trying to figure out how and what would save our marriage, he had already removed himself emotionally.

After listening to him express his reasons for divorce, I immediately did a rewind in my mind and began walking through memory after memory to try and find some hint of when it was that I'd stopped pleasing this man. *"Michelle, I want to take care of you for the rest of your life"* was to play over and over again in my head throughout our divorce proceedings. He had promised me! Promised never to leave me, never to walk out on me, always to be there for me. What about those promises? So I turned the accusations on myself, wondering, *Where did I go wrong? How could I have done something different?* Mixed in with the questions was some guilt, because after years of fighting for something that obviously wasn't there, I had to admit I felt some relief. Then, I felt fear. After the reality that we were getting a divorce began to set in, the questions quickly changed to *What will I do? How can I live without him? How will I sleep alone at night?*

My former husband, the father of my four children, had been slowly closing me out of his life—physically, emotionally, and spiritually—for several years, and now it was all over. Just like that. I'd invested my life and everything in my soul and entrusted it to this person, and with the quickest stroke of the pen it was over.

Final Thoughts

Now you know a little of our stories. But how about yours? Do you hurt so badly in the middle of the night in that now all-too-empty bed that you literally think the pain will kill you—and sometimes wish that it would? Do you find your-self thinking, *Who came up with divorce anyway? Obviously, it wasn't someone who understood what it means to have your heart ripped out of your chest!*

The train of divorce may have been coming at you from a distance, barely visible, for a long time. Now it's right in front of you, barreling down larger and louder than you could have ever imagined. You see no way of escape, no exit. You see nothing but true hopelessness and despair, for you are not in control of someone else's decision. You just get hit full force and dragged along the tracks for the ride. Hang on, Sister. This too shall pass!

It's okay to feel shocked. It's okay to feel pain. Nothing prepares you for the knock-the-wind-out-of-you sucker punch of "I'm not sure I ever loved you. I want a divorce." You may have even known you were heading toward the "Big D," or you may even have been the one to utter those words, but the shock still comes. We don't care if you and your husband have been fighting for twenty years and you hate each other's guts, it is still shocking and earth-shattering when you are told the words, "I want a divorce, and I mean it!"

It doesn't matter how long you have been married, be it one year or thirty. Just look at anyone who has experienced losing a child through miscarriage. The length of the preg-nancy doesn't matter. Death is death, and it is still over-whelming. The baby may have only been ten weeks along, but his parents already had names, a vision for the nursery, and a valedictorian speech all imagined. Then, in one brief moment, the dream is gone.

Divorce, too, is like a death. In some ways, it is worse. It hangs around like the stink of a skunk on a country road in July. It will probably cross your mind that death would actually be easier since it would be more final. With death, eventually there is closure. No one chooses to die, like someone is choosing to divorce.

Welcome to the first stage of grief as it pertains to divorce: shock. It won't be your last stage. Like psychiatrist Dr. Elisabeth Kubler-Ross noted in her famous "Five Stages of Grief,"[2] which include Denial, Anger, Bargaining, Depression, and Acceptance, along this train ride through divorce, you will also have pit stops at the stations of denial and depression (Goody, goody, right?) before arriving at the ultimate destination of acceptance. Some of your stops will be longer than others. You may even backtrack to a stage you already visited once or twice. Don't give up hope. Keep moving forward, and hang onto Jesus. He will see you through.

The final stages of grief are acceptance and, with God's help, forgiveness and healing. To survive your divorce, it is very important to understand that you have suffered a death and that you will fluctuate between all of these stages. Divorce ranks as the second-highest cause of stress after the death of a loved one, according to *The Unofficial Guide to Divorce* by Sharon Naylor.[3] Please understand the stress you are experiencing is completely normal. Part of the shock of divorce itself may be the shock of hearing, "I don't want you anymore, and I really don't have a great reason." You are unable to control what is happening . . . you can't fix this, you cannot change another person.

Embrace your feelings at this time. You must let yourself grieve before you can heal. And you will heal. Right now, you are a broken woman, wondering, *Why? How? What?* But the day will come when you will be whole again. You will; we promise. Now repeat this phrase:

I will live.
I will laugh.
And, yes, I will love again!

Five Fruitful Steps You Can Take During the Initial Shock of Impending Divorce

1. Pray and ask God for direction and strength to make it through. He will walk with you through the hard times and carry you through the unbearable times.
2. Consider your options prayerfully, especially if your husband has already made the choice for you to divorce. Will you fight it? Wait calmly and pray it through? With the help of those who love you, formulate your response and game plan.
3. Find someone "safe" and "neutral" to talk to—preferably a pastor or Christian counselor. Try not to use a family member, your attorney, or anyone of the

opposite sex, as you are too vulnerable in many ways right now. Also, *do not* confide in your children. They are still your kids, not your friends. And their dad is still their dad, no matter what!

4. Remember to do all you can to take care of yourself physically, emotionally, and spiritually. Try to keep comfortably busy, and stick to some kind of routine. Write it down, find an accountability partner, do whatever it takes to stay healthy so you are not adding sickness to your heartache.

5. Seek out those who will help you. Now is not the time to play the "Little Red Hen" who can do it all herself! You need time to cry and time to absorb the blow you've been dealt. Have someone take the kids to and from school, take a weekend away, do whatever it takes for you to safely come to grips with your new reality.

Survival Checklist

The Basics

❋ *Breathe*—Breathe in and breathe out. This seems simple for the rest of the world, but we all know it's not very easy for you at this moment.

❋ *Cry*—Allow yourself to cry without guilt, but remember to try and dry up the waterworks in front of the kids.

❋ *Eat*—You must eat. We know you don't have an appetite, but you will pass out if your blood sugar drops. Carla has the ambulance ride bill to prove it.

✳ *Sleep*—Sleep will be nearly impossible, but you must give it your best effort. Your eyes will look bad enough from the crying, much less the bags that will develop with sleep deprivation.

✳ *Say "no"*—Keep your routine, but don't volunteer for any extra stuff. Try to get out of any big commitments like supervising the second-grade Christmas pageant. You have enough stress right now. The last thing you need is sixty seven-year-old children hyped up on candy canes and parents calling you to ask why little Jacob couldn't be one of the angels.

✳ *Survive*—Really, we mean it! Satan may plant some really bad thoughts in your head like, "Your children wouldn't have to come from a divorced home if you aren't here." Get those ideas out of your head immediately, and know that God will help you through this. We are living proof!

Chapter 2

Alien Abduction–Denial

"I will never leave you nor forsake you."
—*Hebrews 13:5 NKJV*

Well, now that you've faced the shock, you ask yourself the $64,000 question: *What in the heck happened to my husband?* The choices are obvious:

a. Someone cast an evil spell on him.
b. His brain went on vacation.
c. He was abducted by aliens.
d. He got hit in the head with a [insert appropriate sport for your hubby] ball, causing his mind to snap.

If you selected (c) then you feel like we all did—that he was surely abducted by aliens. This thinking leads to the conclusion that, more than likely he will return back to Earth during the process or even after the divorce is final and realize the wonderful new life he so desperately wanted lacks something: *you!*

You may be hoping that by then you'll be echoing Carole King, able to march up to his face and sing, "Well, it's too late, baby, yeah, it's too late . . ." Or maybe you fantasize that you'll make him grovel a little (okay, a lot), but when he's on his knees you will agree to forgive and forget—then fall into his arms for a mad, passionate making up and making out session.

Ha! That is so not likely to happen, ladies. It may be true for Disney characters and in the occasional Hollywood blockbuster romance, but in real life the fantasy rarely becomes reality. In real life, after the initial shock of the announcement that he wants a divorce, has moved out, or has taken up with someone else hits you head-on, the next stage in your emotional process is most likely going to be denial. You simply refuse to admit the truth or face up to this new reality.

If you really think about it, you may find that all through your marriage, you and your spouse swept feelings under the rug, thinking that by doing so you'd avoid conflict. You denied your true feelings. You hoped that with time, things would change. That's what we all do. Perhaps if couples would face their feelings head-on and deal with these issues earlier, judges wouldn't have calendars jammed by divorce cases waiting to be settled.

The reason we don't confront problems is because we don't know how to deal with conflict positively. Most of the time it causes more distance between us because we don't know how to resolve our problems effectively. Now hubby's denying the truth about how his decision to leave you will affect you. And you're denying the truth that he is really leaving at all! If there is cheating going on, he's most likely thinking with his body and not his brain, if you know what we mean. He thinks the new babe is the answer to everything he has been looking for and that she is his last chance at happiness. If he's not cheating and just wants out, he's probably convinced you'll both be better off without each other. He has completely lost his ability to reason properly.

Before you chime in with a "Yeah, that's true!" remember you're not much better off. You may be thinking that if you make his favorite foods, lose ten pounds, dress seductively when he comes to pick up the kids, or tell him it was all your fault, he will suddenly realize what he is losing.

In the denial stage, we tend to pray we will wake up from this endless nightmare that the marriage is ending. We try to convince ourselves the aliens will bring our husbands back intact and hope they'll realize what they are doing to us and the children. We tell ourselves that they won't go through with it, that when they wake up tomorrow they'll see the light. But tomorrow never comes. The man we trusted with every fiber of our being has turned out to be, well, a lot less than Prince Charming. How could it be? How could we have been so fooled? Was it all an illusion?

Connie

"The Aliens Messed with the Wrong Italian"

If you, like us, have received the ultimate blow and are trying to figure out which way to turn next, you're probably scratching your head and wondering, *What happened to the man I married?* You're looking at him, and his voice sounds the same, and he appears to be the same, but this clearly isn't him at all. Perhaps he's had a twin you didn't know about all these years. I refer to this horrible discovery as "The Alien Abduction." Yes, some spaceship has come down to Earth, kidnapped your beloved husband, and dropped down a clone—an exact replica of his physical self, but not really him.

I remember looking at my husband and saying, "You look like Fred, you sound like Fred, but you're not Fred. Who are you? Or are you the real Fred, and you just pulled off lying to me for twenty-six years? My Lord, you deserve an Oscar!"

I think that was the real $64,000 question for me: Was he just faking me out for the last twenty-six years trying to be the man I wanted him to be? Was he that good at hiding his feelings from me and our family and friends? Or did he really just change within a week's time? Because the man I left and said good-bye to the day I took our daughter to her internship was not the man I returned home to one week later. I still don't know the answer. Only God knows for sure.

Where was the man who had given me the twenty-fifth anniversary card (just ten months before he left me) that said: "Your face is the first thing I want my eyes to see when I wake up in the morning. I love you very much, and I'm looking forward to the next twenty-five years with you." Just one year later, when we were separated and in the process of a divorce, I received a bouquet of flowers and a card that said: "I know I've hurt you, and I will have to live with this for the rest of my life."

Usually, the alien abduction point is the point of no return. By this time, they've most likely mulled over in their minds their plan of leaving you for quite some time. They've made their decision, and it's final. I realized that my husband was at the point of no return the day he came home from work and I tried to hug him; when I tried to put my arms around his neck, this veil seemed to come down over his face. He looked expressionless, like Data on *Star Trek: The Next Generation*. He pushed my arms away from him, and I knew at that moment I'd really lost him. I was just attempting to hug the clone the aliens dropped off.

The second confirmation came when my younger daughter tried to contact him to no avail for a few days, simply because the real Fred would've returned her phone call immediately. The alien didn't. And when she did finally get him on the phone, she found out he was with "her" in her hometown just one state over from where we lived. My daughter laid into him, saying things like, "Who are you? Don't you realize what you're doing here? You're cheating on your wife!"

Even with these confirmations, I still believed the aliens would bring the real Fred home.

If your husband has left you for another woman, it may even cross your mind that she may be the only one who could knock some sense into him. While that is possibly true, it's about as likely to happen as winning the lottery. My older daughter, using an age-old tactic, wrote the "other woman" a letter imploring her to let go so we, her parents, could at least get into counseling. She enclosed a copy of the vows he'd said to me on our wedding day. That didn't do the trick. In fact, Dad responded in anger, saying, "How could you throw a knife in Wilma's heart like that? She doesn't have a mean bone in her body." *Helllooo?! What planet are you on? What about our hearts?*

Many of our friends who had known us since college and knew we were the loves of each other's lives met with him, imploring him to give our marriage a chance. His family was devastated, and they tried to reason with him as well. Our friends and family all asked him why he didn't come to them earlier and why he had not told them about his un-happiness before he made the decision to divorce. He of-fered no answers to any of us.

I even had this crazy thought of calling the other woman

on the telephone myself. But I knew it would do no good. In his mind there was no turning back, and talking to her would only fuel the fire. My final card was a spiritual one, giving him all the Scripture references on divorce and once again begging him to reconsider for the sake of his own soul. He simply said, "This isn't helping me."

Family and friends who knew us over the years all said he was just going through a severe midlife crisis, and surely he'd come to his senses before "going through with it." We were the model couple. All of our friends wanted to be just like us. We made each other laugh, enjoyed being together, and rarely had disagreements. But looking back over our marriage I see now that having no disagreements was not necessarily such a good thing. You need a good knock-down, drag-out discussion every once in awhile. Otherwise, things build up over time and suddenly you are hit with that freight train (or the alien abduction) right between the eyes.

I can honestly admit, now that I am divorced, that I am jealous of people I meet who have been married for over twenty years. I think to myself, *How did they make it work? Why did I fail? Where did I go wrong? What could I have done differently?* While it is natural to go through a period of denial, this is the time to own up, girls. Take a long hard look at yourself and assume your end of the responsibility for why your marriage failed. In reality, it's not *all* his fault. I can honestly say in my case that my former husband seemed happier in our marriage when the girls were little and I was home being a full-time mom and taking care of the house. When I started showing an interest in other things and started working, our relationship wasn't as strong.

Too, my being a perfectionist could've been more of a minus than a plus. And in my case, sarcasm may have been an issue. It wasn't so much what I said, but the way I said it. My husband told me that he was leaving me because he thought I was "mean." Translation: Chicago Italian. I was direct and to the point. Very emotional, full of passion, sometimes blunt. But never mean. At least I didn't mean to be.

I'm not trying to minimize his feelings. Perhaps from where he stood, I was mean. Maybe he found that part of my personality charming when we were dating, but on a day-to-day basis, it got on his nerves. He later retracted that statement and replaced the word "mean" with "insensitive."

Looking back, I see that I was in as much denial as he

CONNIE'S LIFE LESSONS
The Denial Stage

The dilemma in denial is this: Perhaps we do want to face the harsh reality that he's leaving and not going to change his mind about coming home, but by doing that, then we feel like we're giving up hope and not trusting God for a miracle to happen. We feel that facing the truth is like giving up hope. The crucial question is: When do you look at the situation for what it truly is and accept it's not going to change? We must eventually face the facts. If his mind is made up and he won't give God an inch to move in the situation, then things are probably not going to change. As hard as that is, we must accept it and move on. Moving forward is usually a good sign that you're leaving denial behind.

was. I loved him very much, but I wasn't completely happy in the marriage. There was a huge void. Many of my needs weren't being met. In fact, I could see we had grown apart. I certainly wasn't the same person I was when we first got married. From a spiritual standpoint, we were in completely different places. That doesn't mean I was better. It just means we were different. I didn't address these issues with him because I thought I was being picky and that he wouldn't understand—that he'd be defensive with me rather than listen to what I was saying. I tried to accept him with all his faults and tried to look at all the positives in him, which was a good thing in some ways. I guess I expected him to look past my faults as well. After all, we'd vowed to stay together "for better or for worse."

I totally regret my lack of communication with him. I have learned a huge lesson . . . the hard way. Success in a relationship can only be achieved by being completely honest and telling the truth.

Carla

"June and Ward Cleaver Never Talked about Divorce"

"No!"

It's the first word anyone says when faced with a horrific pronouncement. Your favorite TV show depicts a policeman announcing to a mother that her child has been in a car accident, and the mother screams, "No-o-o-o!" Your girlfriend tells you her father has just been diagnosed with cancer, and you say, "Oh no, I am so sorry." You've just caught your children diving into the brownie pan, and with chocolate on their faces, they tell you, "No, Mommy. We were born with these brown stains all over our cherubic mouths!"

Denial is a defense mechanism to protect us, in a way. I remember a time when I was younger and visiting my dad during summer break. My little three-year-old brother, a.k.a. "Tiger Woods," accidentally hit me between the eyes with a metal golf club. Had the concussion not been so traumatic, I might have laughed at the toddler running around the yard screaming, "I didn't do it! I didn't do it!"

In many ways, divorce is no different. One partner doesn't want to admit that it's happening. The other will not own up to the fact that his or her new friend *is* more than a friend and that there is, indeed, an affair. For hours, days, weeks, months, we tell ourselves this isn't happening. We may gradually admit that it's "serious" this time, but we really won't allow it to sink in. Again, this is our mind's way of dealing with the trauma: *If I tell myself it's not happening, then it won't happen.* Perhaps we delude ourselves, too, by thinking "mind over matter" will conquer all.

For me, denial lasted about a month. I recall shaking my head and just murmuring, "No, no, this isn't happening to my family. This is the worst imaginable thing; it happens to other people, not me."

Coming from a divorced home, I had planned from a very early age that I would find a good Christian man one day, and we would have the "perfect" family. I swore that *my* children would never have to deal with split holidays and stepsiblings. I met my husband at the tender age of sixteen, and during our six-year courtship through high school and college, I couldn't have been more sure that I was marrying "the one." For goodness' sake, we were married in the same church both of us had been baptized in! He had to be the perfect one that would never sin and leave me, right? Wrong. We all sin. Neither of us was perfect.

Fast-forward to my thirty-first year, now married to my high school love and mom to a four-year-old and a two-year-old, and my husband calls it quits. We were flopping, and there wasn't a thing I could do about it. As I look back, I strongly believe I was influenced as a child by episodes of *Leave It to Beaver* and by role-playing with my Barbie dolls. I married the Beav, and I tried my best to be Barbie. Here's the kicker: he left me *after* I dropped fifty pounds and looked more like Barbie!

On the outside of our marriage, everything looked perfect. Being in marketing and public relations by profession, I was our family's publicist. From the Christmas newsletters to the beautiful family pictures I orchestrated every year, we were the picture of happiness and success. I was so good at my job that when an old friend received a much shorter letter and picture of three of us, instead of all four, he actually thought my husband had died. I called to clear up the

matter, and he said he was in shock. He would have believed that a death had taken place before a divorce.

All delusions aside, if you had asked me to tell the truth
about the state of my marriage before my former husband's "announcement," I would have had to tell you we
were in a constant state of mutual contempt. I couldn't
honestly say he was the love of my life at that time. Travel,
jobs, and heartache over the years had taken its toll. Regardless, I still wanted to make it work. I was a "fixer," and
surely I could fix us. Talk about denial.

I didn't even want to admit there could be another
woman. It took my pastor (yes, my pastor) to say that "No
man leaves his wife and small children after so many years
without something or someone else to run to." I was in-
structed to go home and look around. I finally did, and
there it was in print: not only on the cell phone bill, but also
on our home phone bill. When I confronted him, my husband said they were just friends and denied there was any
type of inappropriate relationship.

I regrouped and huddled down to formulate my next
play. I was determined to be strong enough for both of us
and determined that I could forgive him anything—anything—for the kids and to keep our life together.

Imagine this scenario: He's come home just long enough
from his flight schedule and his "friend" to change clothes,
see the kids, and repack. I have cooked his favorite beef
stew, cornbread, the works. Mary Chapin Carpenter's ren-
dition of "Come Grow Old with Me" is playing in the back-

ground. As he is leaving, I beg him to consider counseling. He practically laughs in my face. I beg him to not talk to his "friend" while we are trying to work things out. By this time, the children have run upstairs and are, unfortunately, watching this scene unfold from the balcony. He yells back, "I'll talk to whoever I want, whenever I want." So, of course, I scream back that if she is such a great friend, then she can come clean the nasty toilet where he's just been due to his "nervous stomach." (I wonder why?)

Girlfriends, I shudder as I recall this. I feel so stupid for trying to make it work and hoping that they were just friends, stupid for begging, stupid for yelling in front of my babies.

And talk about a glutton for punishment! Each time he was away, I would concoct another scheme to get him back when he returned. Because he would return, right? I read every book I could find on marital crises, from Christian living to counseling titles. My favorite, of course, is the one about the submissive wife that I saw on Oprah. I thought perhaps I was all wrong in my approach. Instead of fixing him, I would work on me. He would see the effort and remember what we once had.

I became so desperate in my search to find the cure that I even tracked down the author of the submissive wife book and called her at home one night. I wasn't worried about being arrested for stalking because this was too important. My life and my children's lives were at stake! I begged a complete stranger to talk to me at ten o'clock at night so she could teach me how to practice what she preached so my husband would fall in love with me again and come running back. I should have known that the chances were slim when the author gently noted that we can't make someone love us and that if he had left, then it was probably too late.

Bless her heart, she was probably thinking of that movie *Misery* with Kathy Bates, where the obsessed fan actually kidnaps her favorite author and then breaks his legs so she can have him all to herself. I praise God that this was before the days when most people had caller ID or I may have ended up in the slammer. I can see the headlines now: "Distraught Wife Stalks Author."

My shenanigans continued as I rallied the troops and enlisted family and friends to help me make him come to his senses. From his sister to his father with a heart condition to numerous friends, I thought for sure that peer and family pressure would help. This, too, backfired. His family pulled away, proving that blood is thicker than water. Friends started to distance themselves from the situation, claiming they couldn't pick sides. I even had one set of friends block my phone number. The husband forbade his wife to talk to me. It turns out they were having their own set of problems, and since he was also a pilot, our situation must have struck pretty close to home.

The icing on the cake was when I also tried the age-old ploy of writing a letter to the "friend." Despite having found pictures of my husband and some girl scuba diving,

CARLA'S LIFE LESSONS
The Denial Stage

The denial stage is a roller-coaster. You let your hopes build, thinking that something, anything, will change his mind and send him running back to you. You may pull out all the stops to win him back. Get wise counsel during this stage. Surround yourself with family and friends who can lovingly say "enough" when you are throwing your self-worth over the cliff trying to gain his attention. Let God have control, and see whether or not He brings your husband back. It will be His loving hand that guides your husband back to you or that same loving hand that cradles you if you remain headed for divorce.

plus the discovery of Honda car keys in his pocket (we had a Toyota and a Ford), I still wanted to believe maybe they *were* just friends. (Note to self: This much denial equals *stupid.*) As per my Christian counselor's advice, I was told that writing this letter would be a therapeutic exercise and that I didn't have to send it unless I wanted to.

Well, of course, I had to send it! I was in a war to save my family, and I would enlist even the help of the enemy in this battle. I halfway begged, halfway accused, and halfway tried to guilt her into leaving him alone. (I know that adds up to 150 percent, but who's counting at a time like this?!) I remember writing: "If you are really his 'friend' then you won't let him throw his family away." And the letter worked, though not the way I hoped. It turns out that despite the fact that it was addressed directly to her and that she had a rather unique name, the letter was "mistakenly" opened and posted on the bulletin board at work. (Yes, I mailed it to the office since I didn't have their home address.)

I received a call one afternoon while the children were napping. I was reading the latest *How-to-Save-Your-Marriage-You-Stupid-Idiot* book when my husband called. My gut still wrenches as I recall the venom with which he spoke. He did not suddenly have fond memories of our life together. He had definitely not changed his mind about coming back. Instead, he described the embarrassment "she" had suffered and the fear he now had of losing his job. He closed with words I will never forget—words that awakened me from the fog of denial I had been living in.

"I'm coming to get the children. I don't care what happens to you. *It's over.*" Then he hung up. I think he was afraid that I was so on edge that I might even be capable of hurting the children if I could do something as desperate as sending that letter.

For me "de Nile" had been so much more than that big river in Egypt that the Israelites crossed after God miraculously parted it. For me, it was a way to maintain a façade that had now truly crumbled beyond repair. It was only once denial was left in the past that the pathway to healing could begin. But I didn't know that for a long time.

Rosalind

"Divorce Doesn't Happen to Christians, Does It?"

I didn't want my marriage to be over, and because I was in denial, I kept trying to convince myself my husband was coming back. In my mind I kept thinking, *We are only temporarily separated so we can deal with our own issues, and then God is going to bring us back together again.* I was so desperate and so desirous of finding a way to bring him back that I fasted and prayed for several months. During that fasting period, I lost a lot of weight, which led to family and friends being concerned about me and what I was eating (wondering if I was eating or not). I, of course, told them not to worry and never shared with them that I was fasting for my marriage, for fear they might think I was crazy.

Was I? Was I crazy to want my husband back so much that I would do anything to get him back? I kept begging God to bring him back home, to help him to see the light, to reveal to him all he was losing. My son needed his father, and I wanted my husband back home where he belonged. Conflicts? Sure, there were conflicts in our marriage, but what marriage doesn't have conflicts? I admit, I said some things that were hurtful, but what wife or husband hasn't said things they regretted later on?

The day before we went to court, he called to check on me to see how I was feeling about the next day. I had to take one last opportunity to try and win him back. I shared from my heart and told him I didn't want the divorce. Again, he said that he had to be obedient to God. And then he began to cry. (Puh-leezzz! Whose voice was this guy hearing, and who was really in denial here?) Crazy as it may sound, we were both crying on the phone, and I was still holding out hope.

I told him I had to go because I was going to be late for my Bible study at church. I cried all the way to church. Even after arriving at church, I could not contain myself, but I realized I had to get it together before I walked into the classroom, so I tried to calm down. But when I walked into my study and saw all my friends, I broke down again. My Bible study teacher stopped the class and prayed for me right there.

Sisters, that night was so painful for me. I had to tell the class that I was going to court the next day because my husband and I were getting a divorce. I was truly so overwhelmed with the thought and reality of what was going to take place I could hardly hold it together. And I wanted God to fix it.

When I got home, I received a phone call from a gentleman at church. He told me that he had gotten a message regarding my situation, and he felt led to call and pray with me. I thanked him, and I thanked God. I couldn't believe someone would call me from a church where I wasn't even a member. I really felt like the Lord was letting me know He was going to fix the situation. He had people praying for me and interceding on my behalf.

The next day I made my way to the courthouse. I was still praying until the eleventh hour for a miracle, and

ROSALIND'S LIFE LESSONS
The Denial Stage

If you are in the denial stage of your recovery, it's okay. Just don't stay in that rut. Even though you may be fighting the idea of divorce, you can and should take this time to develop your relationship with God. Find out who your identity is in Him, not in your husband's eyes or estimation. I came to recognize that God can take the pain I was experiencing and use it for my good. You can, too, but you have to be open and willing to allow Him to heal you so that you can move on.

somehow I really thought one was going to occur. When I got to the courtroom, I found out our hearing was not scheduled for that day. Immediately, I thought it was my miracle. God was intervening. He was going to work it all out. I had asked God to show me a sign, and He had.

Both attorneys were perplexed because they couldn't believe the twist either. Then our lawyers consulted with the judge for ten to fifteen minutes. I was praying all the while for a cancellation, but they decided to go ahead with the proceedings.

Girls, I was so disappointed! My heart ached. I had truly thought God was going to change everything. He was going to perform a miracle and give me a wonderful testimony of a marriage saved. But this was not the case. (Instead, I have a testimony of a life saved, a life of survival and God's faithfulness. But we'll get to that part later.) All I could think of as I sat there was, *God, why is this happening to me and my son? Why?*

When the judge made her final statements, I fell apart. Tears rolled down my face, and I couldn't hold back my emotions any longer. I will never forget my husband turning and looking over at me with this blank stare on his face as I sat weeping, tears streaming down my face. Still, the same questions and thoughts kept racing through my mind. *I knew I had issues I needed to work on, but I couldn't have been such a terrible person. How could the man who told me he loved me and wanted to spend the remaining days of his life with me divorce me? Those words were part of our wedding vows. What about what we did in December for our anniversary? We both upgraded our rings because we were determined to make it work. What went wrong?*

Even after he moved out of town, I was still living in denial and hoping somehow my husband would change his mind and come home. It wasn't until I decided to get some serious help that reality kicked in and I finally realized he was gone and never coming back. Although I never shared with my family and friends about my fasting period, God used all of it for good because it made a huge difference in *my* walk with Him. I learned through counseling that I was not crazy for wanting my husband back so desperately. I was not crazy for feeling the way I felt.

Ultimately, the divorce recovery group and my counseling played an important part in my life because I was able to leave behind the painful shell that had caused me to be blinded to the truth. I had to become spiritually and emotionally healthy for myself and for my son. I realized it wasn't just about me. I had a little boy who was affected by this horrible tragedy as well.

Michelle

"Just Not Ourselves Lately"

We've all heard people say, "I'm just not myself lately." Of course, when we're under major stress and our lives are falling apart, it's pretty obvious we won't be at the top of our game. Not only do the thoughts cross your mind that an alien has possibly abducted your husband, but also you begin to wonder if somehow, while he was visiting, that alien did a number on you as well. There were many times during the course of it all I said things I didn't mean, many instances where I did things I would never have done under normal circumstances. They say divorce is like the ripping of one flesh into two. I believe it. I think when your heart and soul are being ripped from you, it is pretty normal for you to feel "not so normal."

I will never forget sitting across the table discussing the final details of the divorce with my former husband and thinking to myself, *I don't know this person. This is not the person I have spent the past fifteen years of my life with.* It really is like an "alien" kidnapped him one night while I was sleeping and replaced him with a person doing a bad impersonation of him. In our final discussions, when I would sit staring (okay, glaring) into his eyes, searching for some sort of familiarity, I'd find nothing familiar staring back at me.

During our divorce proceedings, he returned the allega-
tions, claiming I, too, was not the same person he had married fifteen years earlier. The fact of the matter is neither of
us was the same person we'd married. Hopefully, any two
people who marry will change for the better as time moves
on. What we were really saying was, "I am not happy with
the person you have become. I am not happy with who you
are now." He no longer liked my weight, my laugh, and the
fact that he thought we didn't have the same interests in life.
I even found out in the midst of our divorce that—all these
years—he had hated the way I decorated the house.

Had he been holding all these feelings in? Suddenly, every
negative feeling he had for me felt like it was being thrown
onto me like an ugly, worn-out blanket, smothering me until
I couldn't breathe. Where was all of this coming from? Who
was this person, and who had taken away the guy I knew, the
guy I had spent thirteen years in marriage with and fifteen
years getting to know? Where was he?

It felt like somehow I was living someone else's life. I was
definitely "just not myself lately." I kept thinking this nightmare would vanish, and my life would resume as it was when
things were good between us. I remember after our divorce
waking up many mornings momentarily forgetting I was in
fact divorced, and looking around for familiar things from
our old house and our room we had shared together. It
would take only seconds for me to realize that I was alone
and in the house I had moved to with the kids. All I had built
with this man over the past thirteen years was gone. In those

moments, I would remind myself over and over about the four reasons I had to go on, the four reasons I had to learn to somehow live again: my children—Josh, Aaron, Madison, and Jacob. But in those beginning stages it was never easy.

My former husband suddenly became a cordial acquaintance. How strange is that? This man I had made love to, had children with, spent holidays with, was suddenly someone I used a completely monotone voice with and never cracked a smile at. Someone I couldn't even look in the eye for fear I would break into tears in front of him, someone who seemed callous and so far away. Divorce is a strange thing. You sign papers saying you are no longer married, but you still have to wait some time for your feelings to actually follow what has been legally settled.

Although my things were now in another house, I still somehow could not accept the reality of my situation. My mind knew it was over. I knew I needed to set the boundaries and not continue to put myself through an emotional hell. But my heart, or my ideals, or some part of me didn't. It was still Denial, with a capital "D." My counselor had highly recommended I keep my confrontations with my former husband brief and have nothing to do with him except for when it came to the divorce proceedings. He went on to tell me that even if my husband decided to go to counseling or decided he wanted me back, letting down my boundaries and making myself a doormat would only be damaging to my kids and to me.

But for some reason, I felt sorry for my former husband.

I kept thinking how hard things were on me and how surely they must be the same for him, if not worse. This is my gift and my weakness, girls: mercy, mercy, mercy. Even at the expense of looking like a fool. My husband had moved on. He had already mentally removed me from his life, and here I was trying to find ways to help him when I could barely take care of myself and our four kids. It was not my job to worry about him and try to fix things. This was his decision, and he would learn to live on his own just as I was having to.

Of course, looking back on the situation, it is so easy for me to tell you to just let him fend for himself.

But I know you are probably asking, "How do I do that with someone I have spent a large portion of my life taking care of?"

It was hard for me to let go, and it took some painful events before I could finally make the decision to do so. I would cook meals and have the kids take them to him just to make sure he was eating well. I went over and cleaned his house a few times because I just knew he needed my help (Wrong!). But the worst thing I did during the divorce process was that when he needed me, he would call and ask to come over and "talk." But our talking would lead to other things, and before I knew it he would be spending the night.

I would let him stay over, thinking somehow it would change his mind about me or maybe somehow it would open a door for us to get back together. Instead, I would wake up and feel used and depressed to the point of contemplating

MICHELLE'S LIFE LESSONS
The Denial Stage

Looking back, I am amazed when I think of the power my then husband had over my life—a power I so willingly gave him. With just a few words, he could completely derail me. This is a time when you need to be strong and set boundaries to keep your emotional state from worsening. Hang in there, girls; it will be quite some time before you can actually sit in the same room with the man you called your husband and feel okay with it. This moment is different for everyone. For some it takes years before things feel "normal" again and you are able to discuss things amicably. For some it may never happen. For the sake of your children and for the sake of your heart healing, my hope is that each one of you forgives and lets go.

suicide. Ladies, if your husbands want you back, it won't be because you are sleeping with him. You did that when you were married, and it didn't keep him bound to you. Ultimately, it will only cause more hurt and damage if you emotionally open yourself up to him over and over again. And it keeps you firmly living in the Land of Denial, unable to move toward the healing God wants to give you.

It wasn't easy for me. I continued to live with the hope that there was still something left, that somehow he would come back and want our family to be together again. When I would make dinner for the kids, I would—without even thinking—set the table for six of us. My kids would gently remind me I had set the table for one too many. Eventually, I would get it right.

I just couldn't imagine the holidays alone. At Thanksgiving and Christmas I found ways for us to be together as a family. I kept hoping maybe he wanted to be together, too. After all, he agreed to come over. (Of course, I had given him the guilt trip of how important it was for the kids to "feel" like things were normal.) I was trying to fix things myself instead of leaving it to God. Things weren't "normal," and all I was doing was delaying the healing my children and I so needed. My efforts to orchestrate because of my denial left me feeling more rejected and my children feeling more confused.

Final Thoughts

When you move through the denial phase of the grief cycle, you can finally admit the truth about what is really happening and start looking to the future. You can take control of your life and what happens now. God will not abandon you. He will walk with you through this mess (and so will we). He will give you the strength you need to go on. Again, we remind you: You are not alone. Even though all of our circumstances are different, we've been where you are, or at least in the same neighborhood. Life will go on. You will hear the birds sing again, and the sun will shine again. We know you're in the thick of the storm right now, but remember, a rainbow follows: "Weeping may endure for a night, but joy comes in the morning!" (Ps. 30:5 NKJV). So repeat after us again:

Write your own letter. Get it all out on paper. Address it to your soon-to-be-ex-husband or the other woman if one was involved, whatever works best for you. Express yourself freely. Tell it like it is, and say exactly how you feel, including all of the "Why's?" Pour your heart out; write every little detail. This is your pity party. (We advise having plenty of chocolate on hand for this exercise; it will help sustain your energy.) Now, here's the important part: Don't send it to anyone! Gently fold it and put it away for safe keeping. You will need it after Chapter 3. You can be the victim all you want in your letter. Then, after that, forget it. Exit the Land of Denial, and start getting on with your life.

I will live.

I will laugh.

And, yes, I will love again!

Five Fruitful Steps for Moving Through the Denial Stage

1. Make the conscious choice to—in the words of Nike— "Just Do It!" Move out of the place of being the victim and into the place of overcoming. Repeat: "I will live and not die" (see Ps. 118:17) over and over again.

2. Make lists of your blessings, putting on paper what

you do have instead of dwelling every moment on what you no longer have.

3. Ask God to give you a clear picture of where your marriage really stands. Is there really a chance for reconciliation? Whether there is or not, don't put your life and your children on hold waiting for it to happen.

4. Listen to those who love you. They can probably give you a clearer picture of where you stand—maritally, emotionally, spiritually—you name it. The trouble is you may not want to hear it. You may want to preserve your delusions. Remember that the family members and friends who love you are on your side. They are not telling you things just to hurt you. They are speaking the truth with love.

5. Leave your husband alone. Ooh, this is a hard one! During the denial stage, it is all too easy to try to take control, win him back, or even seduce him! Don't do it! Don't call, send cards, or drive by his new place. Leave him alone, and let God deal with him. Only he (with the Lord's help) can make the decision to repent and return. All your nagging, whining, begging, and throwing yourself at him will just embarrass you both and plunge you straight from denial into despair.

Survival Checklist

Breathe—Continue breathing and take it one day at a time. You will one day be victorious.

* *Exercise*—Get into a good exercise routine and work out your frustrations.

* *Cry*—Once again, it's perfectly okay to cry. It cleanses the heart and soul.

* *Dwell on other things*—Don't dwell on the state of your marriage, because, believe it or not, there are other things in your life that need attention.

* *Get help*—Continue talking to a professional. You need this time of help. Again, be careful about entrusting a friend of the opposite sex or commiserating with a gentleman in a similar situation, because this will only lead to a very unhealthy relationship (more on this later). You are paying your counselor to hear your sad song, and this is good because he or she will help you change your tune.

* *Indulge*—Do something nice for yourself every day. Indulge with fresh flowers, get a massage, take a nap. You will need all the energy you can muster and all the pampering you can afford. If you can't sleep, go to the health food store and ask if they have anything natural to help you. There are relaxing bath oils and sleep aids available.

* *Pray*—This is a time to draw closer to the One who created you.

Chapter 3

Reality Sets In–Anger

"My dear brothers, take note of this: Everyone should be quick to listen, slow to speak and slow to become angry, for man's anger does not bring about the righteous life that God desires."
—*James 1:19-20* NIV

Okay, so shock and denial have come and gone—for the most part—and now you realize that all the future hopes you had of you and your former husband retiring, lounging without a care in the world in your rocking chairs, watching your grandchildren run to and fro in the meadow, have—*poof!*—vanished. All those dreams are now ashes at your feet. You find yourself instead dreaming of ways you could possibly destroy his life. You may find yourself sitting alone in a rocking chair, clutching a teddy bear, crying uncontrollably (or eating uncontrollably), and entertaining thoughts like, *I hope he gets some fatal disease, dies, and the kids and I get to live off the life insurance. Better yet, I hope he contracts some disease from the new S-O (Significant Other) and is suddenly thrown into a state of remorse, comes knocking at my door, begging for me to take him back. At which point I laugh in his face and shout, "Never!"*

Your thoughts may not be as extreme as these, but if they are, that would be totally normal based on our experience. Each of us, at some point during our divorce, had thoughts of revenge—however un-Christian-like—running through the back (and front) of our minds. Each one of us had different reasons to be angry, different levels of feeling it, and even different ways in which we worked through it. But in the end it was all the same process. The ultimate goal is to let it go.

It is perfectly normal for you to be angry in your current situation. We all were! But it is one thing to entertain thoughts that come out of your anger and another thing all together to dwell on those thoughts or take action on them. The key to our healing has been to embrace our anger, face it head-on, deal with it, and eventually get rid of it. It's kind of like getting up and facing the freight train, grabbing onto it and determining to ride that sucker until it runs out of steam. It won't roll over us; we're too tough.

So one good thing that anger can do is get you out of "victim" mode and get you moving again. You just want to be moving in the right direction. And, sisters, revenge ain't where it's at. Fueling that anger and allowing it to control you, especially when you are in the negotiation process with your former spouse, will hurt you the most. He can use your anger against you and also become so angry himself that he fights you even harder. We are human, and we will get angry, but we must remember in the long run it only hurts us, our children, and our families when we continue to live as victims long after our divorce is past. Refusing to let go of our past and move on can be as devastating as the divorce itself.

Michelle

"Dying to My Dream"

Girls, I had a dream, just as you once did. Years ago I dreamed of a beautiful wedding that would join me and my soul mate, with whom I would share my life. I dreamed of children, grandchildren, and all the joys that go with the whole package. Divorce was never an option. We would devote ourselves to each other through the good times and the bad, even to hell and back if that's what it took! I tried to do everything by the book. I made sure to introduce him to my parents and didn't marry until I had their blessing. We waited a good two years before we married. I had an hour-long ceremony to honor God for my wonderful day, and most of it was worship to thank Him for bringing me a husband.

If there was a checklist of the right things to do before

you marry, I think I would have qualified for hitting them all. Never in my life would I have dreamed up what would end up happening.

I'm not sure if I was angry at him for quitting on us or for his part in destroying my dream. After describing my assessment of our marriage to my counselor, he replied with words that really hit home for me. "Michelle," he said, "is it the loss of *him* you are so desperately devastated over, or is it really the loss and disappointment in having to die to the dream of all you wanted your marriage to be, and to the dream of marriage itself?"

Wow! Those words hit me strong! I thought about them for a moment and realized my counselor was right. I was angry with my husband for destroying my dreams, and I was angry that I couldn't fix it!

Looking back, I remember the guilty-but-sort-of-wonderful feeling of utter relief I had when he told me he wanted a divorce. Our life had been chaotic for so long. I had spent the last few years striving to find any way I could to "fix" our problems. I had unsuccessfully tried to get us into counseling. I had spent hours planning the perfect vacation, only to find not even a beautiful location could change his heart toward me. I'd cooked, I'd cleaned, I'd even offered to quit my job, only to find out later he had been planning to leave me so it was all in vain.

Now, I spent months allowing those tormenting thoughts to enter my mind: *Why? Why didn't he fight for me?*

and *What? What made him stop loving me?* Even as I write these words, tears well up in my eyes as I remember all too well how rejected and lost I felt. In my experience there is no feeling I can think of that is worse than the feeling of not being wanted, the feeling of true rejection both physically and emotionally.

Out of my disappointment and devastation as a result of my divorce came a realization of hidden anger I had harbored. The last year of my marriage, as my husband distanced himself both emotionally and physically, I had unconsciously blamed God for my pain. If you would have asked me if I was mad at God, I would have replied, "Absolutely not," but my heart eventually revealed differently. I associated God with the failure of my dreams. I felt as if He could have, and should have, changed my circumstances. After all, I had been praying! I had prayed for years about our relationship. I had spent many nights in bed, with my back to my husband, tears streaming down my face, silently enduring the pain. Crying out to God and begging Him to help me, begging Him to give me wisdom on what to do.

I stood by watching my children suffer because of the situation, again crying out to God and asking Him to relieve us in our pain. There were countless nights I would gather the children up out of their peaceful sleep and feel like I had to leave our home. And all I could think of was, *Where are you, God?* I felt like screaming at the top of my lungs to see if He would scream something back. There

MICHELLE'S LIFE LESSONS
The Anger Stage

The day I was able to get past my anger was a big day of freedom for me. Ironically, at the same time I experienced this freedom, I also moved to a new house on Freedom Court, in a sub-division called Liberty Hills. This was no accident. Freedom was all around me! I no longer was in bondage to my anger at my former husband, nor was I in bondage to my anger with God. I will say that there are moments still when I think back on what happened and have feelings of anger, but those feelings no longer rule me. I am free.

was only silence, blackness, and questions.

It took me a good six months to work through my anger with God. I wrestled with Him; I called out in my pain, asking Him to give me answers, to make some sense of this hell I was living in, to just give me the reason why—why this had happened to me after all I had done to live for Him.

I stopped going to church. Why should I? I was angry and didn't want to hear a message, nor read one. Those well-meaning friends who sent me Christian books to somehow make me feel better would have been disappointed to find them thrown in my garage somewhere. I was in a faith crisis for the first time since I had accepted Christ twenty years before. I had given my life to Him in a radical way, letting God know I would do *anything* He asked of me. I would spend my life preaching the very gospel that so radically saved me from the depths of hell I had been living in. Now, twenty years later, I was baffled to find myself crying once again, "Save me, oh God, from myself, from my pain, from my despair."

Today, I cannot even express my regret in pushing God away from me. I have cried many a tear over this. He is the one true lover of our souls, of my soul, and yet I could not embrace Him in my time of crisis.

Connie

"From Cherished Vow to Business Transaction"

The day my former husband moved out of the house was the day reality set in. Suddenly I could no longer remain in denial. That was the day that I stopped begging for forgiveness, stopped blaming myself, stopped groveling and moaning, and just got good and "torqued off"! Some people get torqued off. I got good and torqued off. I was so angry at him for betraying me, rejecting me, and abandoning me. What happened to the commitment, the vows we made to each other before God and our family and friends? What happened to the sanctity of marriage?

What happened to the "for richer or poorer"?

The "for better or for worse"?

The "in sickness and in health"?

Rage was now brewing inside me. This is the time during the separation and/or divorce process when you may be mad at God. Now, I knew God could change my husband's mind. However, I wasn't mad at God for not changing it, because I know God gives us all free will. He doesn't make us do anything. But I was angry at God for letting me marry him in the first place. If He knew I'd go through all that pain, I thought, then why did He let me marry him? Then I thought, if I hadn't married him, I wouldn't have had my two precious daughters. And I realize now it is because of them that a part of me will always love my former husband. A part of him is in my girls, and for them I'll forever be grateful.

I knew that anger was a normal stage, but I really prayed that bitterness wouldn't set in. I prayed about everything, and yet still, the anger crept further in. And I found myself sometimes praying that bad things would happen to my husband. Not horrible things, but things like hoping he would be unable to perform sexually with his new love. Can you believe I actually prayed that? God had to get a good laugh out of that one. Thank goodness He has a sense of humor.

I remember one particular night when we'd been separated for a month and he asked me out to dinner to discuss our future together. We hadn't talked or communicated for that entire month. I really thought a miracle might have occurred and maybe, just maybe, he would come home and agree to some counseling sessions and try to make "us" work again. I got all dressed up and looked pretty good (in spite of the swollen bags under my eyes due to lack of sleep and crying 24/7). It was in the middle of the summer, so I went out and bought myself a brand-new short black skirt with a pretty lavender sleeveless top. I had lost weight (the only perk of going through divorce), and I wanted to look gorgeous. My makeup and hair were flawless. When he saw me, he even commented on how pretty I looked and reached over and stroked my arm. I wanted him to tell me he'd move back in and give counseling a try. Instead, my hopes were shattered again.

He said he filed for a divorce, and I would be receiving the papers from his attorney within a few days. Then he asked me the famous question: "What do you want?" And I thought, *What do I want? I want you, of course!* At that point I angrily told him, "You are a despicable person, and the sight of you makes me sick."

Immediately following my comment, our waiter brought the beautiful dinner we had ordered. (Nothing like a good, hot dinner going to waste!) I couldn't eat after what he had just told me. I told him I needed to leave, and I'd

CONNIE'S LIFE LESSONS
The Anger Stage

Anger left unchecked can be destructive, but righteous anger can also be a great motivator. After the initial shock, a little anger can get you moving in some new, practical directions. Taking constructive steps to protect myself and my kids financially during this time was important—not to exact revenge, but to be able to survive. Anger helped me stand up for myself and the assets I deserved from my marriage. As the saying goes, "Be wise as a serpent but as harmless as a dove." Do not make it your intention to hurt, but get educated and stand up for what you need.

think about what I wanted and get back to him. As I left the thought came to me, *I'll tell you what I want. I want to shake you silly and slap some sense into you!*

That evening I faced the harsh reality that a cherished vow from the beginning becomes nothing more than a business transaction in the end when you're talking about divorce.

Carla

"No Hallmark Card for This One!"

Anger is an interesting emotion. It comes on so quickly and with such force! I remember a scene in the movie *Steel Magnolias* when Sally Field, who played M'Lynn, is with her gal pals after her daughter Shelby (played by Julia Roberts in her breakout role) has died. The women are at the burial site after the service. Sally's character is absolutely distraught and, at first, very quiet as her friends console her. Suddenly, she starts screaming, "Why?" as reality sets in about the loss of her precious daughter. Her ranting and raving turns to anger as she recounts the injustice of loss, and it's only when Olympia Dukakis offers up Shirley MacLaine as a punching bag to literally absorb some of Sally's emotions that Sally realizes her irrationality, and some comic relief ensues. In the film, the whole cycle takes only a couple of minutes to ensure the required Hollywood happy ending.

In real life, this stage of grief is a slippery slope that can propel you backward and forward. Just when you think the anger is under control, it bubbles up like hot lava, threatening to erupt.

After my husband railed at me for writing a letter to his new friend is when the lava of my anger started to boil. Because at that very moment, I realized that he truly did not care about me anymore. His concern was for her and our children. My time of denial was swiftly over as I contemplated the last fifteen years of my life, the bearing of two children through difficult pregnancies, and the supporting of our household while he earned his flight hours. Heck, I even got him his first flying job at the company I worked for. Plus, his dream company called him for an interview after I sent the CEO a letter pleading on behalf of my "wonderful, loving husband and father." He had only been out of training for a few months, and here he was leaving me and telling me he didn't care what happened to me.

So there I was . . . ready for round three in the heavyweight championship of divorce and the five stages of grief! Chuck the denial. Leave "de Nile" as that river in Egypt. Bring on the anger!

To show you the depths to which my anger went, I want to admit something to you. Something shameful I will forever regret, but which is important to relate so you can see you're not alone in your feelings. On September 11, 2001, a couple of weeks before my papers were to be signed, for a millisecond I actually hoped that it was my husband's plane that had been hijacked and crashed into the Twin Towers in New York. I want to cry now just thinking about how horrible that thought is—to want your children's father to be dead at all, let alone during such a traumatic time in our country's history! But I did think it. There were other dreams and horrid thoughts, and I knew these were from the pit of hell itself. I thought I had made progress when the dreams went from death-by-plane-crash to simple scuba diving accidents—*not!* I had to constantly pray for forgiveness for the paths my angry thoughts took.

During our difficult journey through divorce, it seemed like my husband knew how to push my every button during every interaction with him, whether on the phone or in person. It was a weekly torment. I asked my counselor why my husband had to continue to hurt me and make my life miserable. Hadn't he done enough? My wise counselor told me that when people turn their back on everything they once believed, they have a lot of self-hatred. And the only way to make them feel better about themselves is to make the other person feel bad. In his mind, it would justify his infidelity. The nicer and more loving I was, the harder it would be for him to rationalize his actions, and the better it would be for the children and me. Somehow, I had to reach way down deep and through prayer and petition to God, find a way to put aside the anger.

I knew my counselor was right, but this task is *much* easier said than done. Taking karate classes and distancing myself from him helped. Also, instead of talking to him, I let him leave his messages on an answering machine. I tried to make the "child exchange" as brief as possible. The true test came one night when he brought the children home and gave me a bag of hand-me-down clothes from the other woman's child. (Keep in mind that our divorce was still not final at this time.) As we stood there in the parking lot, I could feel the lava brewing as my sweet son exclaimed that he had met the child *and* his brother *and* their mother! My little cherubs were jubilant, but a thousand

CARLA'S LIFE LESSONS
The Anger Stage

Anger can actually be a good thing, as you go from the numb zombie who won't admit the truth that her marriage is ending to a brokenhearted woman who is actually allowing herself to feel. It hurts terribly, but somehow you know you are getting closer to recovery from your nightmare. However, you can't linger in the desert of anger for too long, or else you will be on the road to becoming a very bitter, dried-up old woman. I knew this would not be good for me or for my children, or for any prospect God would bring in the future.

thoughts raced through my mind of things I could say to this man who was systematically ripping my heart out:

a. "Tell that woman I don't need her stupid kid's clothes!"

b. "You have got to be kidding if you think I'm gonna take clothes from the woman who broke up my home!"

c. "Thanks." (Let's be practical . . . and loving. We need this stuff. Plus, the kids are watching.)

Today, I praise God that I chose (c), otherwise known as the "high road." I admitted to my Sunday school class that I didn't think Hallmark made a card for this: "Hmmm, thanks for the clothes; you can have the husband." But as we went through the bag, I found myself thinking things like, *Wow, here's a Land's End winter coat and some Tommy Hilfiger items!* I'm not a brand-name shopper, but as we continued to look through the items, I began to think I had gotten the better end of the bargain. She could have him; I'd take the clothes. Now, that's what I call progress!

Rosalind

"Praise Jesus! Roz Didn't Have a Gun"

Was I angry? Yes, there were times when I was angry, when my life was turned upside down. I didn't know if I was coming or going. I went from having my own home daycare so I could be with my son to having to go out looking for a job because my financial status changed overnight. And it was not by any choice of mine! Angry? Oh yeah, baby, I was angry. When bills were due, and I didn't know where the money would come from to pay all of them, I was *angry*.

When my husband left, he left me with everything—house note, credit card bills, car note, you name it. It was obvious he wanted *out*—wanted a fresh start. The problem was that meant leaving me with all the baggage. I felt like he was looking out for himself and it didn't matter if my son and I had to bear the burden of his freedom.

Stressed? You bet I was stressed. I would work all day and then have to go home to even more responsibilities. There were many times I was just too tired to do anything. I had to force myself to get things accomplished. My life was in so much transition, and I felt out of control. Everything was so overwhelming.

I have to admit just saying I was "angry" would be an understatement. "Full of rage" would better describe my feelings when I found out my husband was involved with one of our acquaintances from church. I found it inconceivable that this other person could even be capable of aiding my husband in the destruction of our home. Never! I still remember confronting him about the affair I knew he was having, and even with all the evidence I had discovered, he still completely denied it. The love letters, the flowers she received on Valentine's Day—the same Valentine's Day he gave me a lousy CD (and I don't mean the kind of CD you get at the bank)! Yes, I was angry. I felt betrayed, rejected, abused, embarrassed, humiliated, ashamed, and abandoned. You name it, I felt it.

Don't believe me? How about this: As it turned out, the acquaintance moved away. When she did, my husband started hanging out with someone else. I saw him with this other woman all the time so I began to assume *she* was the

other woman, especially since my husband had never admitted to having a relationship with the acquaintance who
moved away. Because I saw them together a lot, I got
curious—I wanted to know the truth. So I found out where
she lived and showed up at her doorstep to confront them
both. They became afraid and called the police. It wasn't
like I walked up with a gun or anything. (However, I admit
some terrible thoughts did cross my mind.) The police arrived and asked me to leave. I told the police officers I was
there to see my husband.

After leaving the scene, I was so furious that I contemplated making another attempt to confront them both at
church the next day. When I arrived at church, my thoughts
were far from worship. They were all about wanting to get
even. I could just hear the breaking news headlines: "Major
fight takes place between a ministry leader and his wife during church service."

Walking into church, I noticed both of their cars in the
parking lot. I began searching every section of the church
and couldn't find them. I knew they were there somewhere,
and I was determined. All I could think of was getting my
rage and frustration out. I had thought about it all night and
was ready to explode!

I ran into one of the associate ministers' wives, and she
noticed immediately how angry and upset I was. We began
talking, and I shared the depth of my pain over what had
taken place the night before. She was so sweet and gave me
the best advice, sharing with me how it was not worth it,

and how the battle was not mine but the Lord's. While her advice was good and so what I needed to hear at the time, my heart was just not ready to receive it. I was so determined to find some satisfaction of revenge I didn't want to see the truth.

As I approached my seat in the sanctuary, the pastor's wife came over to me. She, too, immediately noticed my rage. Again, I shared my horrible experience, hoping for some sort of affirmation of my anger. Instead, she placed her arms around me and shared with me those same words the associate minister's wife had shared: "This is a battle for the Lord, and it is not your battle to try and fight. The Lord knows of your pain and frustration. Let it go."

ROSALIND'S LIFE LESSONS
The Anger Stage

You will feel betrayed not only by your husband but also by others. Remember, it is not their fault. There were times when I could do nothing but think of how I wanted to destroy the lives of those who knew this affair was going on and never told me. This is extremely difficult to forgive, but people are not perfect. You may have thought others would embrace you and help you get through this nightmare. Some will, and some won't. If the church knew how to handle marriage crises well, perhaps there wouldn't be so many marriages on the rocks. Look to Jesus for healing, and ask friends for support. Be clear about what you need, but try to accept their limitations if they can't provide it.

"It is so hard for me to let this go," I replied. "I am so tired of him hurting me."

Remember that letter you wrote in the last chapter? The one to your spouse or his new friend, the one that cataloged all your hurt and disappointment? Find it and pull it out. It is time to release all of that anger. Feel free to burn the letter, shred it, or destroy it in any manner you choose. Now, don't go burning it with all of his clothes, pouring gasoline on it and torching his car like the beautiful Angela Bassett did in that chick flick Waiting to Exhale, but do get rid of it. As the letter goes away, visualize that you are letting go of all the resentment, hurt, and pain. If you hold onto it, you are the only one who will be hurt by it.

Again, she said to me, "Let it go; it is not your battle." At that very moment, I broke down and wept in her arms. She held me tight and went on to share with me how much she admired me for enduring and persevering through my tremendous heartache. She also shared how many people in our church saw me as a great witness because of how well I had responded to my circumstances. She gave me one last piece of advice, asking me to keep my head turned to the hill from whence cometh my help, because all of my help came from the Lord (see Ps. 121:1).

I did not approach my husband and the other woman that day, and today I am glad.

Final Thoughts

Dear, sweet friends, let us tell you a secret. Until you are able to stop asking yourself the questions of why, what, and how did this happen—until you are able to stop meditating on the many things "he" has done to you and your children—you will be unable to let go of the anger that inhabits every part of your being. You will *not* be able to live again and build a new dream for yourself until you are truly able to let go of the dreams you once had. It is the difference between existing and actually living. Our hope is that you will choose to live again.

For each one of us it was different. The pain you are feeling is real, just as our pain was real. Our anger was real—and we had the right to be angry! You have the right to be angry, but don't *stay* angry! Anger is a real part of the healing process, and you can't go around it; you have to go through it. But make sure you don't live in it and make it a part of who you are and all you are to become. While you are working through, never forget to keep pointing yourself to the light at the end of the tunnel, by repeating to yourself:

I will live.
I will laugh
And, yes, I will love again!

Five Fruitful Steps for Putting Aside the Anger

1. Keep any interaction with your spouse short, sweet, and to the point. Do not get embroiled in rehashing history or waste your energy fighting a battle you can't win. Communicate through your attorneys if you have to, but remember that this gets very expensive very quickly!

2. This one's hard but worth it: Practice saying your spouse's name, then repeating, "I love you with the love of the Lord," again and again. Ask God to channel your burning anger into something positive.

3. Use the anger-fueled times of extra energy to get organized, whether it's filling boxes to prepare to move or tracking down paperwork you will need. Ask the Lord to help you be productive, not destructive, with your burning emotions.

4. Take deep breaths and count to ten—a lot! Deep breaths really do release a feeling of peace, as do walks outside. Pray for self-control, and ask God to put a muzzle on your mouth!

5. Read all the verses you can on anger and on the tongue and mouth. Get a good look at how destructive the tongue can be. Words can destroy what it took years, even decades, to build. Don't poison yourself or your kids through your rage. He can move out of the way of your anger, hang up the phone, or drive off.

You are stuck with yourself, and your kids are stuck with you, too! Remember that: "A gentle answer turns away wrath, but a harsh word stirs up anger." (Prov. 15:1 NIV).

Survival Checklist

* *Express*—Tape some old pictures of your former spouse on a punching bag and punch away. (Do *not* let your children see you doing this or allow them to participate.) This will help you express the frustrations you're feeling without acting out that anger in a destructive manner!

* *Protect Yourself*—As Connie suggested, this is now a business transaction, and you should treat it as such. Get a good lawyer to protect yourself.

* *Scream*—Feel free to go out into the woods and scream at the top of your lungs. It really does help!

* *Vent*—Feel free to have venting sessions with very close, trustworthy friends when you are so filled with anger you are afraid you might do something rash. Work through your anger with a counselor if you can. Make sure you are talking through all your feelings, so they don't stay cooped up inside you.

* *Try a Massage*—Go on, go for it. Get a massage. You'd be amazed at how it can help relieve the stress and anger you carry inside. Who knows, maybe you could get massage therapy as part of your divorce settlement (smile).

❋ *Read God's Word*—Try the book of Job, if you really want to feel better about your circumstances. He suffered more than any one human being should. Watch how Job handled his anger and circumstances. It will truly bring peace to your soul.

❋ *Pray*—Pray for strength and wisdom. Get on your knees daily, and pray without ceasing everywhere you go. You might look like you're talking or constantly mumbling to yourself, but everyone expects you to be a bit "off" right now anyway (smile), and the running conversation leaves the door wide open for the Lord to keep working in you.

❋ *Repeat*—Finally, keep repeating our mantra: I will live, I will laugh, and yes, I will love again! This may feel silly, and so far from the truth, but you're getting closer, we promise!

Chapter 4

The Plague–Depression

Answer me speedily, O LORD;
My spirit fails!
Do not hide Your face from me,
Lest I be like those who go down into the pit.
Cause me to hear Your lovingkindness in the morning,
For in You do I trust;
Cause me to know the way in which I should walk,
For I lift up my soul to You.

—*Psalm 143:7-8 NKJV*

Congratulations! The divorce path has now led you steadily down the road and straight into the pit stop called Depression. (We say congratulations, because you truly are getting closer and closer to becoming healed. It just doesn't feel like it yet!) This is what many people consider the most difficult stage of grief. It's a time when you're likely to eat like you're expecting triplets or not eat at all. It's a time when you're either sleeping for hours on end or not sleeping at all. It's a time when you may have difficulty thinking clearly or concentrating. It's a place where no dreams exist, unless they are nightmares. It's a place of hopelessness and, to be completely honest, it's a very dark, frightening place to be.

That is the nature of depression. Dear friends, we who have all gone through what you're going through have been in this black hole, this seemingly bottomless pit. And we have made it through to the other side. Do not despair. This, too, is a normal part of the grieving process, and we'll tell you right up front that the worst thing you can do is to isolate yourself from others.

You may be so depressed you can't function with day-to-day activities. Even getting out of bed may be a chore. Caring for yourself or your children or going to work may as well be a big mountain you've been asked to climb. Several of us—Carla, Michelle, and Roz—all had children ranging in age from babies to middle school during our divorces and had to put aside our despair the best we could to manage the daily tasks children require. You may be in the same boat, having to rely on friends or family to help with the kids during this time.

One woman Connie met in her Divorce Care class told the story of how she had relocated to a new city with her husband because of his job. She had no family or friends there and wasn't even familiar with the city. Four months after the move, he left her and filed for a divorce. She had left a great job, lifelong friends, and a home she loved to support him. Now, here she was. Thanks to his "new-found life," she was forced to start over all by herself.

That's one of the reasons it's so important to be part of a good church. Your pastor or perhaps someone in the women's ministries can assist you. They can guide you in getting the help you need. Don't be embarrassed. Pastors and clergy deal with this kind of thing on a regular basis. It's just part of the job.

You may also feel very fearful while in this state of depression. Each one of us had fear and had to fight against letting it overcome us. Connie was so afraid that she felt her mind would snap at any moment. This was just how fragile she was at the time.

This is not necessarily a good time to be watching tragedies on the news, reading horrific stories in the newspaper, or listening to that radio station that plays all the love songs. This *is* a good time to get into counseling if you haven't already, even if you can't afford it. Some counselors will be willing to work with you to fit this very important step into your budget.

This is the phase where you're really going to see what you're made of. You're going to have to do a lot of praying and a lot of self-talking, and you'll need to surround yourself with people who love you and will make you get the help you need. You can do this. You're stronger than you think. You want to survive this. With God by your side, you will!

Connie

"I'm in the Basement, but Where's the Floor?"

I've always been afraid of rides at amusement parks, especially roller coasters. However, against my will during my divorce, I had to ride the emotional roller coaster of shock, denial, anger, and all the stages of grief. It was making me sick. When I began to realize that, barring some miracle from God, this divorce was really happening to me, I had this overwhelming sense of fear.

After all, I had never been alone in my entire lifetime. I came from a large Italian family where all my aunts, uncles, and cousins lived within a few blocks of my house. We were always together. Sunday dinners are etched in my mind. I can still smell my grandmother's spaghetti sauce and meatballs. From there I went to college, lived in the dorm, and hung out with all the girls. I met Fred there, and we were married a year before we graduated from college. I think he married me because of Grandma's passed-down recipes that I'd mastered.

Fred had a large family, and we were around them as often as possible even though they lived out of state. And we started our family three years after we were married and produced two lovely daughters. So, I'd never had the experience of being on my own until now. Fear set in, and it set in big-time. Many questions cluttered my mind: *How will I live alone? How will I do things for myself? What do I do if some-*

thing breaks? How do I work the five remotes he had programmed for one blasted TV? How do I work the stinkin' thermostat? It took me thirty minutes to figure out how to turn on the heat! How will I balance the checkbook and manage the money? Where do I start? Who will take care of me when I'm sick? How can I eat alone, sleep alone, watch TV alone, exist alone? Will anyone ever love me again?

When my husband left, he timed it perfectly to coincide with our younger daughter moving out, too. So I dealt with divorce issues and empty-nest issues simultaneously. All of this equaled a big fat "D." Not the big "D" in "Denial" or "Divorce." I mean the other big "D." Depression. This is where I entered the black hole, a basement with no floor. I felt like I was drowning or being consumed. There was no way out. Or so I thought.

I had been in this place once before, when I went through severe panic attacks after the death of my dad. I can tell you, it's the scariest place to be. It was absolutely smothering. I didn't want to go there again because I was afraid I wouldn't be able to escape.

In the majority of cases, counseling from a good marriage therapist or psychologist is essential in this stage, to help you figure out how to climb out. Some people I have spoken to have had medication to help them manage for a time, to put a floor in their basement. (Speak to your physician or counselor before taking any medication.) In my particular case, meds did me more harm than good. The counseling, great faith in God's Word, and wonderful friends are what finally pulled me out of that bottomless pit.

There were so many "firsts" I had to face alone. I'll never forget that first night in my rather large home, which seemed even larger with Fred gone. I cried all night. I was so afraid. I heard noises in that big house I'd never heard before. I had always cooked dinner and set the table for four people. When he walked out, I set the table for one. Not that I cooked much after he left. It was usually a bowl of soup.

I couldn't believe how lonely and inadequate I felt. I remember one day the pest control man came over to do the quarterly service. I was in the office trying to install a window shade that had just been repaired. I struggled with it and he walked in the office and said, "Can I help you with that, Mrs. Wetzell?" I said, "If it's not too much trouble, I'd really appreciate it." He put it up for me, and I bawled until my eyes and throat ached because I couldn't do it myself.

I felt helpless without my husband. See, I'm "vertically challenged," meaning I'm shorter than the average girl. I used to depend on my husband to reach into the top of the cabinets to get things down for me. Now I had to keep a little stepstool in the kitchen. That doesn't seem like a big thing, but at that point in my life every little thing became a monumental task.

I would be sitting alone watching television or reading a book, and everything seemed *so* quiet. The first time I did my laundry after he moved out, I remember sobbing as I folded the clothes because I actually missed folding his things! He hadn't moved everything out yet, and just looking at his possessions in the house was unbearable. I would walk in his closet just so I could smell him. Imagine that!

Even in the midst of my darkest despair, God's presence was so evident in my life. Six months after my husband moved out, December rolled around—Christmastime, the season of rejoicing. Ha! On December tenth, my divorce was finalized. I didn't even go to court. I had my attorney go in my place. On December thirteenth, I got on a plane headed for Charleston, South Carolina, to attend the college graduation of my older daughter. I had to participate with my "ex" in this wonderful milestone in our daughter's life. So I pasted a smile on my face during the ceremony and the party we gave her. I had to fake my true feelings the whole time.

It was so strange that he and I stayed in different hotels after we had enjoyed so many precious family memories in that charming city. The day after graduation, my ex-husband, daughters, and I went to the market, ate dinner at a quaint little restaurant, and walked through the city. That was the last time we did anything together as a family. On December sixteenth, the movers showed up at my house with two trucks—one for his things and one for mine. Going through the possessions we bought together and then deciding who got what just, well, stunk! I left before the house was empty. How could I walk out of the home we'd built family memories in—the house we'd made a home? But I had to suck it up and do it.

On December seventeenth, I moved into my new little house. One of my sweet friends helped me move in and stayed with me all night. The movers left at two o'clock in the morning. We didn't get any sleep. On December twenty-third, I went up to Chicago to spend time with the girls and my family for the holidays, which were a total blur. All I remember is that I was very sick the entire week at my mother's. I just fell apart. Then I returned to my new "home" filled with boxes everywhere that needed to be un-packed. Thank God for my incredible friends (You know who you are.) who helped me. Without them and my pre-cious Lord carrying me all the way, I'd have been commit-ted to a mental institution.

On New Year's Eve, *my* (former) Fred gave Wilma an en-gagement ring. Six weeks later they were married. I felt like I had endured a severe beating, one punch after the next. Blow by blow, I was dying a slow death.

One thing to remember about this stage of grief is that depression has its own time frame. It won't be over in a day, a week, or even a month. After a while, the heavy black shadow may not sit on you all the time, but it will come back to haunt you periodically, long after the divorce is final and you think you have "moved on" and gotten past all that "nonsense." It's normal—not fun, but normal. Just keep putting one foot in front of the other and asking God to help you keep moving in a positive direction.

The following Christmas, exactly one year after my divorce, was the first year I had to share my children with my former husband. Part of the time they were with me, and part of the time they were with him and his new wife. I had to put up the Christmas tree because the girls were coming to town. Otherwise, I wouldn't have bothered. Normally, putting up the tree was a huge family event the day after Thanksgiving; but this year was another first. I put up the tree alone. Going through the ornament box was horrific. I broke down when I saw all the ornaments that were significant to my husband. I relived Christmases past and once again sobbed like a baby. I put all his ornaments in a zip-lock bag and had the girls deliver them to him when they came to town.

All of these firsts are tough. These are the "ripple effects" that you face after a divorce. They feel more like tidal waves.

During the depression stage, everything plunges you into the pit. Sharing your children with their other parent on special occasions, realizing that your in-laws are now your "out"-laws and that you are no longer a part of the holidays with them. All of these things can create a snowball effect of despair. I loved my in-laws. I'd grown so close to them over the twenty-seven years I'd known them. Now wife number two was with them instead of me. How could I bear it? My father-in-law, whom I love dearly and have a great relationship with, was given a surprise seventieth birthday party around this time. Every family member and

CONNIE'S LIFE LESSONS
The Depression Stage

God has always gotten me through tough times. I have found it to be true that He won't give you more than you can bear. But He also knows you're human and therefore provides you with people who love you. I encourage you to make dinner plans with a friend from time to time. Get out of your house and out of your isolation. Do some normal, social things, even if you don't feel like it. Surround yourself with good people.

all his friends were invited to help him celebrate. My children were there, and so was my ex with his new wife. I wasn't invited because it would've been too weird. I cried all day.

I remember taking my wedding ring off after the divorce was finalized and putting it in a safety deposit box. Instead of taking the ring off, I felt as though I had *ripped* off my finger. That finger on my left hand was connected to my heart, which felt ripped into a million pieces.

One reason depression comes on so strongly is that divorce changes *every* aspect of life. It's much more than the fact that you're now single. Your living arrangements may change. Your job may change, or you may have to go to work for the first time in years. Custody issues with children bring about huge changes. Your financial situation changes. Your friends will change, too, as you lose some who are too uncomfortable now or were more "his" friends than yours, and as you discover others who have walked in your shoes. You may find yourself hanging out with more single women. You may see a lot less of the couples you've always done things with together.

Be encouraged and know that the depression stage does not last forever. You go *through* it. You don't stay in it. You will get out. Remember, God has not given you a spirit of fear, but a spirit of power and love and a sound mind (2 Tim. 1:7). He is close to the brokenhearted and saves those whose spirits have been crushed (Ps. 34:18). God knows you've been crushed and persecuted, cast down but not destroyed. You've gone through the wringer, but you are strong and resilient. You will make it!

Michelle

"Hanging from a Ledge"

For a while, depression knocked me for a loop. Emotionally, I was such a mess that it took everything I had just to get up and go to the store. I could barely make little decisions, much less big ones. One of the most difficult things I faced was going through all our things and moving them into my new home. I had purposely waited until the last possible minute to move. I was so afraid to face the pain that going through all of our belongings would bring. Picture albums from when our kids were born, photos from vacations that seemed like a lifetime ago. The attic was filled with small treasures from the past that piece by piece made up the tapestry of all we had built our lives on. It began to seem as if my life was similar to that of a broken vase, shattered into so many pieces it could never be replaced, or be worth anything again. My life seemed over, finished. Our family was broken, and nothing could change it. (Girlfriend, these are all lies that the enemy would have you believe. Trust me, God does heal the brokenhearted. He does restore the pieces of our broken lives. Do not fear, for He is with you!)

My parents and my brother agreed to help me move. Honestly, I barely remember moving. At the time I didn't care how things were thrown into the boxes, or if they even made it to my new house. I remember barely holding it together as we packed everything and figured out what would stay and what would go, what was his and what was mine. It took every ounce of strength I had. As I stood watching my family load all of the thirteen years of belongings we had accumulated onto the moving truck, the bleak reality of my life again flashed before me. *Somehow, I have to be strong, and somehow, I will get through this* were the continuous thoughts going through my mind.

My kids were counting on me, and yet I felt like I needed someone to count on. Who would be there for me? Who would hold me in my pain? So many nights after my kids would go to bed, I would sit alone on my couch staring out at nothing feeling so helpless, so lost, and so abandoned. I couldn't see tomorrow, nor could I see to the end of the day. Would this hopelessness ever end? Of course it would, but only time and prayer would eventually heal this broken heart.

In the midst of the depression of divorce—or maybe because of it—many women develop a daring, crazy, I'm-going-for-it kind of attitude. Here's an example: I have always been afraid of heights. I can be up somewhere high as long as I don't look down. So when a dear friend asked me to go rock climbing, this wasn't just a little deal for me. It was a great, big deal. I was facing fears. He might as well have asked me to go climb Mount Everest. This was a big step for me, and it took quite a bit of coercing on my friend's part to even consider it.

I don't even look like a rock climber. I am a "girl's girl" all the way, with painted toe nails, makeup, and high heels with a purse to match. Yet I finally decided to go for it. See, there was a time way back in my youth that I was pure tomboy, and I think there was a part of me during my divorce that wanted to be that kid again. The innocence youth holds and the desire to have it back after going through a divorce is somewhat of an oxymoron. You can long to have the innocence again, but wisdom and knowledge does come with the price of experience and age (sigh).

So now here I was on this rock-climbing trip with my dear friend Marcus. He was an expert, carrying the cool backpack that was three times the weight of me and totally at home in woods. He blended into nature. I, of course, stuck out like a sore thumb; I find the woods to be more of a nice place to venture to only for the occasional picnic. The only backpack I carried was a designer brand with my lipstick in it, and I was oh-so-cool in my rock-climbing shoes, cool T-shirt, and some pretty rockin' pants. I was going to fake it 'til I made it up those rocks. My youth was back, and I was "Rock-Climbing Chick."

What a poser I was! Now it was my turn to climb up what seemed like a Mount Everest-sized cliff. It's truly amazing how those cliffs looked so small from a distance. I even remember thinking to myself that it really didn't look all that hard. But when I was right up against that rock wall, suddenly what seemed insignificant from far away was now absolutely insurmountable. All I kept thinking as I was walking toward the wall to start my climb was, *How did I get here? And where the heck is the door out?* Then my pride took over. I was with two other women who also had the three-times-my-weight backpacks. Their bodies looked like the rock I was about to attempt to climb, and I could see no sign of poser in them. I was forced to suck it up and try to look as cool as possible.

The first part of the climb was a breeze. I simply took hold and started clambering up. Every ounce of strength I had was poured into my strategic climb ahead. About halfway up, I came to a stop and suddenly realized that the next part of the climb was vastly different. It was as if nature had purposely designed the cliff to look easy on the first leg to deceive you into thinking the whole thing would be a breeze. My pride went out the window as I began to look like the first-timer I was. How was I going to get past this? This ledge was so difficult, even the more experienced Rock Chicks couldn't get up it without a sweat. I was hanging by my fingertips, approaching the ledge again and again and quickly falling each time.

I was planning my exit strategy, preparing to swallow my pride and ask for someone to go ahead and let me down, when Marcus started yelling at me to not give up.

"I can't do this!" I cried out.

"Yes, you can," he determinedly yelled back.

"You don't understand. I cannot do this, Marcus!"

"I know you can, Michelle," he replied. I realized then that he wasn't going to let me quit. I was going to have to find a way to overcome this huge ledge, or I wouldn't get to the top, and therefore I wouldn't get to go home. It would be dark, and I would have to survive the deadly wilderness alone. (Okay, bit of an exaggeration here, but that's what it seemed like at the time!)

Fine, I can do this, I thought to myself. But my strength, after numerous attempts, had gone, leaving me weaker and weaker. Looking up at the top, it didn't seem so far, but it may as well have been a mile, because I just couldn't see how I was going to make it up.

As I sat there feeling helpless and discouraged by my attempted failures, I suddenly realized this was my life. *This was my life.* I was hanging on a ledge.

I don't know what came over me. Suddenly, it was as if a bucket of tears came out of nowhere and were now running down my face. Here I was, hanging on this mountain I couldn't seem to get up, with Rock Chicks and Marcus cheering me on, and I was bawling my head off. This rock experience suddenly made me realize the level of pain I was in, and the tremendous frustration I felt at not being able to get emotionally past my divorce. It became so clear to me at that very moment that overcoming this rock represented overcoming my divorce. I just sat there and cried for several minutes. In between my cries, I kept attempting to get over this obstacle of a mountain in front of me.

Finally, finally, I was able to muster the strength to conquer. I cannot tell you how I felt when I finally made it to the top of the mountain. I had triumphed over something I never thought I could, due to my fear of heights. I had beaten the mountain and made it to the top. While I had been attempting it, I could hear Marcus yelling, "Go straight up—straight up to God!" When I yelled that I couldn't, Marcus yelled even louder, "Yes, Michelle, you can! You must!" When it finally happened, I had never felt so accomplished in all my life. I knew it wasn't just the mountain I'd defeated. It was much more than that. On that day, I knew I could move on and trust God for my life. I would survive, would get past this horrible hell I was living in. I would somehow live again, laugh again, and, yes, love again. The depression was still there. The pain was still there (still is, sometimes). The heartache still felt unbearable. But I had the assurance that I would make it.

Before you reach your own "mountaintop" experience, you will probably face the worst darkness and feelings of complete and utter aloneness that you ever have felt in your entire life. I felt as if someone had stabbed me in the chest with a twelve-inch dagger and left it there. My stomach was a mess; my life was a mess. Getting through the day was an accomplishment for me. This was so far from my normal personality and temperament that it was frightening. I am a very outgoing person. I love people. I love life. I had never been faced with such depression. In fact, depression

MICHELLE'S LIFE LESSONS
The Depression Stage

You are going to have lots of moments where you just break down and cry. Do it. Don't hold those tears back thinking you have to hold it all together. It's okay to cry. God didn't give us tears for nothing. And remember: "Weeping may endure for a night, but joy comes in the morning" (Ps. 30:5 NIV).

was something I was not familiar with until my divorce. I couldn't sleep at night, I'd either eat too much or not enough, and I had constant, lingering thoughts of suicide. It was as if Satan himself was pulling me into this black hole, and I knew if I gave in I would never return.

I remember thinking that I was such a loser. Seriously, I remember thinking to myself, *I am a loser. Just write the word across my forehead because that is me.* Honey, this is a lie from the pit of hell itself. There is no life that cannot be redeemed. There is no life that cannot be turned around for the good. I am living proof of that. God knew before you did that you would be divorced because He knows all things. He sees all things. He knows the heart of His creation, and it is your heart He is after. If you are in despair, remember He is with you.

I remember feeling as if I couldn't breathe most of the time, as if I was suffocating from the divorce. I felt as if everyone knew and was staring at me thinking, *What a reject!* as if I had some kind of "divorce disease." I wanted so badly to just go and mourn somewhere, to just get under the covers and never come out. But I had four children to take care of. I couldn't just think about myself. Some days were better than others. I remember one night I was so depressed and was still reaching out to my former husband and being rejected again. Crying, I called my friend Mark. While I had done plenty of crying already, the cries this particular night were like none I had ever heard myself cry before. They were from deep in my soul.

Like good friends do, he got in his car and drove five hours to sit with me and listen to my pain. He only had a couple of hours to spare, but it could have been one hour, or even fifteen minutes. Just knowing there was someone who cared enough for me to listen to my heart meant so much to me. For those two hours, I wept uncontrollably. Mark began to sing songs of healing over me. I don't even remember what he was singing, but the music was so healing to my heart. Eventually, he put his guitar down and wrapped his arms around me and just held me so tight. The music and the warmth of a friend holding me brought tremendous healing to me and re-reminded me of my Friend who is also always there to hold me.

Carla

"My Night at the Parthenon (And We're Not Talking Greece)"

The situation seemed so surreal: I was sitting on top of my suitcase in my gravel driveway contemplating the decision I had just made. That decision had been to seek professional help for the hopelessness and complete despair I was feeling. I had gone from being a somewhat confident woman, wife, mother of two, daughter, Sunday school teacher, and former business professional to a shell of a human being who could not stop crying and frankly did not want to live anymore. I kept thinking that if I was no longer here, my children would not have to come from a divorced home. I rationalized that they were pretty young and would adjust well without me.

My identity had been shaken to the core, and the only way I could see out of the mess was to either swallow a bottle of pills or run my car off a bridge. Before this, I had never had much sympathy for people who took the "easy" way out. I always thought life could never be that bad. *Wrong!* Here I was, Miss Judgmental with a giant plank in her eye, now sitting on her suitcase, waiting for a ride to the local "looney bin," aka the Parthenon. I guess somewhere inside I knew I needed to stick around and live, for I did have enough sense to recognize I needed help quickly. Praise God for that psychology minor in school!

I was also very thankful for our insurance program. I couldn't see anything funny about the experience at the time, of course, but as I look back on it now, the name of the program—"Clear Skies"—was hilarious. I recall sitting at orientation at my husband's new company before he had started his flight training. The benefits department went over all of the insurance options, and I laughed at the "Clear Skies" mental health program. I only envisioned needing it for one of the kids if they got mixed up in drugs during the teenage years. Little did I know I would be the one looking for "Clear Skies" just a few months later.

When I decided on the Parthenon, I knew Dorothy wasn't in Kansas anymore. The first clue was the fact that they asked me to bring a suitcase even though I was only coming for a short "consultation." (With a name like the "Parthenon," maybe I was thinking there might be a connection with Greece after all. Perhaps there was a little vacation in my future? And at $1,600 a night, I sure wish it had been a nice cruise to the Greek Isles instead.)

I really was pretty naïve. I think the most difficult part about making the decision was some "advice" I received that if I went through with "this," then I would surely lose my children in court. I was told that I just needed to "get over it." I couldn't "get over it." Heck, I couldn't get under it or around it, much less over it. I knew somewhere in my heart that I had to get through it and that God would show me how. I guess that's why I packed my Bible. And as my dear friend picked me up and drove me to the psychiatric ward, somehow I thought I would be coming home again. My skies were still very dark; and I could barely see through the pouring rain of tears, but I just knew God would provide that ray of hope. Hopefully, I would find my Clear Skies.

Registration was a blur as my girlfriend walked me in and thankfully took charge of the situation. I was a blubbering idiot who could barely give my name, much less any other pertinent details. I specifically remember the nurse, who resembled a Marine Corp drill sergeant, asking me if I wanted something to drink. I could not give her a definitive answer. How pathetic I must have looked as she handed me a Diet Coke. Perhaps that's why they had her do the "consultation."

Sadly, I really was a case. I needed a heavy dose of reality, and that's exactly what I got. Suffice it to say, the body search and confiscation of several luggage items were pretty darn humiliating, and the "suicide watch"

CARLA'S LIFE LESSONS
The Depression Stage

"It always seems darkest just before the dawn." We've all heard that saying a thousand times, but it can be very true. The middle of the night can be the hardest hours of the day, when you feel all alone, and the memories and words of condemnation play themselves over and over in your mind. Take a walk, get on your knees in prayer, turn on some worship music, or take medication, if it has been prescribed, to help you sleep. The enemy is the dark. Jesus is light. It will truly look better in the morning.

by the nurses every hour during the night kind of freaked me out.

During the night, I read my Bible and God revealed many wonderful Scriptures. One that seared itself into my soul was Luke 1:37, "For with God nothing will be impossible" (NKJV). My situation seemed impossible to me, but this verse confirmed that I was not alone and that God was right there with me. He could handle the impossible.

As I lay there in the dark, curled tightly in a fetal position, my mind drifted to the words of the solo I had been rehearsing for the last month at church. It was "I Will Rest in You" by Brent Bourgeois and Michelle Tumes, performed by Jaci Velasquez on the *Streams* project. It's a beautiful song that reminds us of how as children we had ultimate faith in God and how as adults we need to remember that childlike belief, because even though we've grown up, God is still the same and we are still His children. I couldn't remember why I had picked that particular song, but God knew. He knew I would soon need these words to comfort me during a future difficult time.

I prayed all night for some sense of that faith—for the will to live and for God to help me get through this mess and be okay for my dear children. And really that was just what I needed. By the next morning, clear skies were dawning, before I had even seen the doctor! At seven o'clock the next morning, the psychologist came to visit. He was a dear, sweet man who asked me how I felt. I shared with him all of the promises that I'd found in God's Word through the night, that I knew I would be okay, and that I didn't think I needed to be there. Keep in mind that the field of psychology isn't exactly known to be full of believers, but God provided a wonderful Christian doctor who assured me that I was right on target and that he didn't even feel like he needed to prescribe any medication. He said that they would release me as soon as possible as long as I worked with a counselor on an out-patient basis.

Praise the Lord! It would be several hours before I was released, but my sky was already clearing. I was even able to witness to a few patients and nurses before I left.

Now, don't think that one night cured me for life—cured me of all the sleepless, lonely, tearful days and dread of the future. Each new day brought new challenges. I cried so much and wore out the excuse that "Mommy's tummy hurt" when my children asked, "What's wrong, Mommy?" They must have thought I had some dreaded disease. I thank God for my Christian counselor, my church, and all of my dear friends for their support.

Rosalind

"A Woman in Search of Purpose"

Once I got over my feelings of anger (which seemed like an eternity to me), I realized that I was carrying a very heavy load all alone. This realization ushered me right into a state of depression. The transition I experienced was absolutely overwhelming. I remember nights when I had to get up in the middle of the night with a sick child burning up with fever. I had just landed a new job, and my boss was threatening to let me go because I'd missed too many days of work. What was I to do? I had to stay home with my sick baby.

The bills kept piling up, and the money just wasn't there. That's when the depression really kicked in. I had been rejected by the man I thought would love me forever. My self-worth was extremely low, and I really felt terrible about myself. I had a horrible self-image. Let's face it, you don't look in the mirror and see a beauty queen after your husband willingly leaves you for another.

I began to have a very negative attitude about life in general. Depression caused me to be constantly fatigued, with a very low energy level. I had to force myself to do everything because I was so exhausted and worn out—physically, emotionally, and mentally. There were many days I couldn't wait to get home so I could isolate myself from everyone and ball up in a corner and cry my eyes out. I remember friends inviting me over to gatherings at their homes. I would make up excuses because I didn't want to leave my home. All I wanted to do was sleep so that I didn't have to think about anything.

I had a lot of guilt and I blamed myself for the reason why my husband left. There were several times I shared with my mother that I wished I'd been the perfect person because maybe then he wouldn't have left us. My mother tried to comfort me and remind me that no one but Jesus is perfect. She often reminded me how critical I was of myself and that I needed to stop blaming myself for what had happened because it took two people to get married and two to get a divorce.

But overall, I felt like there was no hope. It was not the first time I had fallen into the black pit. A year before my divorce, I had suffered from severe depression. This time, I recognized the signs and was determined to fight my way through it. I vowed I was never going to go back into that state again, for fear that this time I'd lose my sanity altogether.

ROSALIND'S LIFE LESSONS
The Depression Stage

Seek out comforting Scriptures, and post them where you will see them regularly. One passage that really spoke to me comes from Philippians 3:7-9: "But whatever was to my profit, I now consider a loss for the sake of Christ. What is more, I consider everything a loss compared to the surpassing greatness of knowing Christ Jesus our Lord, for whose sake I have lost all things. I consider them rubbish, that I may gain Christ and be found in him, not having a righteousness of my own that comes from the law, but that which is through faith in Christ—the righteousness that comes from God and is by faith" (NIV).

When I went through my first bout with depression, I was miserable with myself because I felt like my life lacked purpose. Sure, I was a wife and mother, but that was it. I'm not demeaning wives and mothers, but I wanted more. I thought I just wanted to be a better wife and mother, but I

Girls, as you work your way through depression, hopefully you have someone who can wrap their arms around you and hold you tight. Just be careful if it is someone of the opposite sex. Make sure that person is someone you can completely trust. And be careful not to cross the line from comfort to sex. It's all too easy to do, and while the affirmation that you are still attractive might be great, the consequences are far greater than the momentary pleasure.

Actually, we would encourage you to stay away from close relationships with the opposite sex completely until you come out of this. We all know how hard it is to stay away from men in this vulnerable time when you are so needing affirmation. We

was really searching for more meaning. I began reading books on balancing my life and how to develop purpose. Now, as I look back, I truly believe God was preparing me for the huge changes I was about to experience through my divorce. He knew what was around the corner. I didn't have a clue.

I have to thank my Abba Father for looking out for my son and me. I know I would not be where I am today and who I am today without Him. I thank God for my obedience to Him, my perseverance, and the prayers of the godly women who were constantly covering me. These factors were keys to getting me out of my depressed state.

all, except for Roz, made the mistake of getting too quickly into (rebound) relationships that were not going anywhere, only to find ourselves digging our way out. As hard as it is, take it from us, don't do it. Take some time to really get through your pain and come out on the other side with just you and God. You need to be whole and healthy again before you have something positive to share with someone else. That time will come, but wait for it. Otherwise you may make a bad choice (or, for that matter, many bad choices) and end up in a bunch of broken pieces once again. Your time of depression will end, but let God, your children, and your best girlfriends be your closest companions through it.

Final Thoughts

Depression is normal, so please don't think you're crazy. You're not! There are so many resources out there to help you cope. Don't isolate yourself. Surround yourself with positive people. Remember, the Lord can heal your broken heart. He desperately wants to. He loves you so very much and He will always be by your side. He will never leave you nor forsake you. Keep pressing, sisters. Keep pressing.

Your pain may be so unbearable that your heart actually aches. It may even cause you to think you're having a heart attack. The four of us can definitely relate to that kind of pain. You may feel like you're hanging on that ledge, hoping you'll find the floor in the basement when you land. You may have cried so hard you don't understand how there could be any tears left in what you think is an empty, hollow shell of a woman. You think you're a loser because you've lost him.

Well, girl, you have to know that this is simply not true. If we could only wrap our arms around you right now, we would. We want to encourage you and let you know you will see the light again. You will wake up to a brand new day. One day soon, you will be able to say, "This is the day the Lord has made; I will rejoice and be glad in it" (see Ps. 118:24). You will have purpose. There will be new goals, dreams, and visions. And if you believe in God's promises, He says He will restore to us the years that the locusts have eaten (see Joel 2:25). Stand on that, dear friend. Whatever you do . . . stand. And keep repeating to yourself:

I will live.
I will laugh.
And, yes, I will love again!

Five Fruitful Steps for Dealing with Depression

1. Do whatever it takes to laugh. Make funny faces at your kids, see a hilarious movie, or challenge a funny friend to keep you in stitches. If all else fails, have

someone tickle you! Laughter lifts the gloom, and it is truly the best medicine.

2. Run to your place of comfort. If home is a safe haven, or your best friend lives in another city, it's time to take a trip. Throw some stuff in a bag and hop a train, bus, or plane. Allow yourself to be nurtured, comforted, and taken care of by the ones who love you.

3. Get a makeover. Nothing pounds our self-esteem like the rejection of divorce. Don't wait any longer to get the nails, hair, or body you've always wanted. Find a salon, visit a spa, set up that manicure, or hire that trainer. Get a facial, or try some new makeup. Call friends over and let them dress you and "doll you up." Aim for a new style that is simple and as carefree as possible, so that you can look and feel good, even on the days when you lack the energy to do much beyond combing your hair.

4. Make yourself get dressed each day, and keep a running "to-do" list. Try writing each night a list of things that need to be accomplished the next day, from reading your Bible to taking the kids to school. If you can visibly see what needs to be done and check the items off as you go through the day, you will feel a sense of accomplishment. You are doing it!

5. If you do not know Jesus as your Savior and have a personal relationship with God, we don't know how you'll be able to really get to the healing stage. God, who created you, who formed you in your mother's

womb (see Jer. 1:5), is the only one who can completely repair you. If you have never come face to face with Him, seek Him now. Just talk to Him. Ask Him to forgive you for all the things you have done wrong, and tell Him you want Him to be part of your life. Then find a good church, a pastor, or a friend you can share this news with. They can help you grow in your newfound faith.

Survival Checklist

* *Surround yourself*—Try to not be alone too much. Surround yourself with good, uplifting, positive people.
* *Get wise counsel*—If you still haven't found a good counselor or therapist, this is definitely the time to find one. Understand it might take awhile to find someone who is a good match for you; don't be discouraged. Ask for a good recommendation from your family doctor or perhaps from a friend who has had good results.
* *Listen*—Listen to classical music or praise and worship songs. Don't listen to music with depressing lyrical content. Sappy love songs are out for now, or you will be the subject of another country and western song!
* *Exercise*—Try to get in a walk or some form of exercise if you can. This, combined with light therapy, is fantastic. Exercise actually releases hormones that make you feel better. So try it; you'll like it. And you'll feel better about yourself.

✳ *Avoid the news*—We suggest you stay away from the news during this season. This is not the time to be hearing about the problems of others and the rest of the world. It can add to your depression.

✳ *Seek help*—If you feel like you want to harm yourself or someone else, call someone immediately who can help you!

✳ *Read*—Read (or listen to) the Word of God. Memorize verses if you can, and recite them. Hide it in your heart. This will act as a "medicine" to your soul.

✳ *Pray*—Keep up the prayer, ladies. Pray, pray, pray. If you have to get on your face before God, do it. Pray without ceasing!

✳ *Repeat*—Repeat the following: I will live, I will laugh, and yes, I will love again!

Chapter 5

Acceptance-Forgiveness Means Freedom

For if you forgive men when they sin against you, your heavenly Father will also forgive you. But if you do not forgive men their sins, your Father will not forgive your sins.

—*Matthew 6: 14-15 NIV*

We've now reached the most important stage in the divorce grief cycle—that of acceptance. It's also one of the hardest to get to, and as Christians, we have found that the only way to get to that station place is through forgiveness. If you walk away with anything from our stories, please walk away with forgiveness. It is the only way hope can reside in you. Bitterness, unforgiveness, and hate cannot reside with love, hope, and healing. You need to forgive not only your former spouse, but also forgive yourself for your own shortcomings and failures.

When you think of your former husband, what comes to your mind? Does the time he gave you the roses on your birthday pop up? How about your first date and how cute he was picking you up in the brand-new convertible he bought just the week before to impress you? Maybe you still have a picture in your mind of his silly little smile and nervous laugh, and how proud you felt when he draped his arm across your shoulder during the chick flick he so graciously sacrificed to see. He did everything "right" on your special romantic first date—from the first moment he picked you up until the last, sweet moment of the evening (when he opted for the "hug move" to prove even further his blossoming love, but also respect, for you). You certainly felt as if you were in heaven.

Maybe those are your memories. Or perhaps your memory drifts back to the first wonderful days (years) of marriage. Like the time he sat in the hospital with you while you were in labor with your first child. He never left your side. He held your hand and coached you on as you agonized in delivering your firstborn. He helped little Johnny or Jackie take their first steps, and he was just as ecstatic as any proud father ever was when that child said the first word: "Da-da."

All right, all right, you say—that is quite enough! We

understand. It isn't easy to look back on your life and choose to think of good memories after you have gone through a divorce. Instead (let's face it, gals), the reality may be more like this: You remember the day he sat down to tell you it was over and how he casually said he didn't love you.

Or perhaps you remember those countless nights you stared so hard and long at his cold shoulder, lying in bed for hours feeling rejected and angry, wounded and alone.

Or how about the times when he shouted at you and you sat there, hands cupped over your ears as if it would soften the sting of his words (or, unfortunately, shouted back).

Maybe he was more subtle, dropping little criticisms such as, "You can never keep it together" or "You need to lose weight—you look awful."

Still other memories may include the first night you discovered the "evidence" or even saw him with another woman, and every bone in your body seemed to shatter. You remember reluctantly asking him if he loved her only to hear the answer hit you like a two-ton truck.

And you remember the faces of your children as they sat and watched their daddy and mommy go at it.

Yeah, those are more likely the memories still being rehearsed in your mind every day. They may still be vivid in your mind's eye. As divorced women, we walk away with whatever monetary things the judge orders, but we also walk away with the "ghosts" of marriage past. When all is said and done and the door of divorce court is closed, none of the monetary things can heal the memories, the wounds, and scars left over from the destruction of your years of marriage. These memories, these wounds, remain boxed up inside your heart. Some of us throw the key to that box away.

Sisters, please don't do that. You need to realize the importance of opening that box up and working through it with the dream of becoming whole again. The fact is if you are to live again, laugh again, and ever love again, then one thing has to happen. You have got to get that box out, sisters. You have to open up that box of memories—the bad memories, as well as the good—as hard as that may be. You have to begin the journey to forgiveness, and it can be a long journey. You don't go through the trauma of a divorce only to wake up the next day and be fine and dandy. But if you hold on to every little thing he ever did to you, it will only keep you from being healed. It will not do anything to him. It won't affect his life or make him see the light. Chances are, he will never suddenly "get it." If you choose to hold on to hate and unforgiveness, then he is actually taking one more thing away from you—your desire and will to move on.

Here's the bottom line: We can't make you, your family can't make you, God can't make you, and your kids can't make you forgive the past! This is a decision and a choice that can only be made by you, but it benefits everyone around you. The choice and decision *not* to forgive is death to your soul. It will keep you in bondage. It will tear you to pieces. Over time, it will rot you from the inside out. That's exactly what bitterness does.

On the other hand, if you are willing to open that Pandora's box, examine the bad memories and set them aside, then concentrate on the good ones (but not to the point of excruciating pain over what you've lost), then you will find yourself approaching the train station stop named "Acceptance."

We know it's much easier said than done, and it will take time. Don't you wish someone could just hand you the gift of a little magic box filled with "forgiveness magic dust" inside, and all you'd have to do is sprinkle it on and you'd suddenly be able to forgive every person who has ever wronged you? Okay, maybe we've seen too many princess movies with our kids. Real forgiveness takes some work. It takes humility; it takes love. It takes the willingness to give up feelings you are absolutely entitled to have, but as a mature adult know will only cause you further pain. God can give you the ability to forgive. It is a gift, and all you have to do is receive it.

That being said, forgiveness is often not a once-and-for-all thing. Acceptance is a process, a journey that leads to restoration. Every little wrong that has been done to you during the process of divorce, every little thing you remember when you think of your former husband, has to be forgiven one memory at a time. Some memories you will find yourself having to forgive more than once.

Acceptance is a decision you have to choose to make

every day until you know in your heart it has been done. Even when you think you've arrived, you will still find yourself in situations where you will need to check your heart over and over again for unforgiveness and bitterness.

Not only is it essential to forgive your ex-husband, but also it is just as essential to forgive the woman he is with now. (Ouch! We know!) And, as stated before, you must forgive yourself. For some of us, it is almost easier to forgive others (well, maybe not the other woman) than it is to forgive ourselves. We want to find someone or something to blame, and it's easier sometimes to place that blame on ourselves and spend the rest of our lives feeling like we need to pay for our mistakes, our failures. The process of forgiveness for us can be even more intricate than the process of forgiveness of a former spouse. Counseling and working through that process is a must.

Michelle

"Broken Glass"

In the midst of my divorce, my weekly Bible study group asked me to share my personal story and to bring an object of some kind that represented my life. My immediate thought was to bring a bag filled with tiny pieces of broken glass. These tiny broken pieces of glass were representative of the tiny broken pieces of my life. The journey I have walked has not been without pain. It has not been without failures and difficulties, but at this time in my life the pain caused by my divorce was the greatest I've ever experienced.

In the physical sense I'd compare it to someone cutting my arm off and walking away with it. The brokenness I felt, the agonizing sorrow and grief I experienced during that time, left this empty hole in my heart. Realizing the hole would not be filled, accepting I would never be able to get my arm and put it back on again, was the hardest thing I have ever had to do . . . other than forgive.

Forgiveness. Well, forgiveness is something I always thought I was really good at . . . until my divorce. My heart had always been able to forgive. I was never a person who could even go to sleep with an argument in process. I had to have some form of closure before I hit the pillow, or I would lie awake all night wallowing in depression or guilt, depending on the situation. I remember after our divorce lying in bed night after night, full of anger and resentment for what had happened. I had never felt this kind of hate for anyone. There had been many people in my life who had disappointed me, failed me, and even betrayed me; but no one had ever gotten to the core of my being. No one had brought me to the place of such utter despair.

The funny thing is I actually hated him for bringing me to the point that I hated him! I felt like going out in the streets and screaming at the top of my lungs, "No! No! This *cannot* be happening to me!" I felt like there was this pain so deep inside me, this anger I just couldn't get out, that I didn't know what to do to release it. I didn't know how to get all the layers of junk I had experienced over the years out of my heart, out of my mind, out of my spirit.

Imagine a layer of concrete over your heart. What could break it away without damaging the delicate muscle tissue underneath? You would have to slowly pick away at it until it was removed. The anger and hatred I had in my heart was the same as a layer of concrete, and it formed there to protect me from the hurt he was causing me. Other layers were deposited every time I focused on my anger and hatred, or even vented them at him.

MICHELLE'S LIFE LESSONS
The Acceptance Stage

We all have our "disappointment lists—the laundry list of things that "he" or "they" did to wrong us. I learned that I had to throw it away. Throw it away and remember it no more. The more we dwell on our lists, the more impossible it will be to forgive. There are days when the list will come back; throw it away again. Remember, forgiveness means accepting that the ones who wronged you may never say, "I'm sorry." You have to forgive them anyway. You may never hear him say he regrets what he did. And you need to accept that and let it go.

Just like you have to pick away at that concrete, you also have to pick away at your hardened heart. You have to slowly pick away at it, slowly forgive. Some days you will gain ground. Some days you will lose some, but until your heart is tender and soft again—until it is exposed—you cannot truly love again. Forgiveness is a daily choice and a choice we must push ourselves toward.

You might be saying, "Girl, I can't forgive him. You don't understand what he did to me! You don't understand how he treats me still." Remember—forgiveness is not about him; it's about you. It isn't even *for* him; it's for you. Do you think he is going around wondering if you have forgiven him?

We all feel justified when we are angry, when we are bitter. We're thinking, *I have every reason to hate him/her! They deserve to be the object of my hate!* Of course they do, but that is not the point. Of course I had my reasons behind the anger and resentment I had gradually built up in my heart over the years. Have you ever met a person who had hatred, bitterness, and unforgiveness who didn't feel justified? Well, I felt justified, too. But being justified doesn't mean that holding on to hate is the right course of action.

I also felt powerless to control those feelings of hate and anger and I knew I had to go against my feelings in order to forgive. The "feelings" of forgiveness didn't follow until much later. Acceptance is not about feeling; it is about a decision.

Even when I apply all of the things I am telling you, I still find myself in moments and situations where I once again have to choose forgiveness over anger. It really is a lifetime decision. The only way I can keep doing it is by being reminded of my own shortcomings and how often I am forgiven by my heavenly Father. The power of forgiveness is found in the conviction of God's Word. It is only in reading the Bible regularly that I find myself convicted of my own sin. Then I am reminded of the grace extended to me, and I can forgive not only him, but also myself.

Connie

"Nursing a Grudge"

"Connie, I want you to forgive him," God said to me one day.

"What, Lord? Are you serious? You want me to forgive a man who has betrayed me, rejected me, and abandoned me?" I responded indignantly. (He was probably rolling His eyes at this point and thinking, *Yeah, I'm quite familiar with that betrayal-and-rejection thing.*)

"Yes, daughter, you must forgive him, or you'll be in bondage for the rest of your life," my Lord replied.

Still, I argued back. "But, God, it's not humanly possible for me to do this on my own."

I wasn't getting out of it that easily. "I'll help you," He said quickly. "Just give it to me."

Letting go of feelings you want to nurse is tough. I love my Italian heritage, but we are great at holding grudges. It's one of the things we do best. I can tell you that my grandma didn't speak to her sister for twenty years because she said something to my dad when he was a little boy that hurt his feelings. Grandma and Aunt Mary finally made up a few years before they both died, but they wasted two decades being angry at each other. So I, being a product of my heritage, still wanted to argue with God. I wanted to try to obey. I wanted His blessing, but was thinking, *God, you want me to forgive a man who has disrespected me and broken our sacred vows. Why can't I just hate him a little (okay, a lot) longer?*

I think if my dad had been alive when Fred left, he would've called "one of the boys" to pay Fred a little visit, if you know what I mean (smile, or at least a grimace, here).

Over the years, I've had to forgive myself for things I'd done that I was ashamed of. I've had to forgive my parents for things that happened in my childhood that caused some damage. I've had to forgive my siblings for little incidents that rubbed me the wrong way. But forgiving Fred was one of the hardest things I've ever been told to do by God. Plus, since there was another woman involved, I had to forgive her, too!

To be completely honest, I still have to give this over to God almost every day. It's an impossible task for me to handle on my own. But someone once told me something that really made sense. Just be *willing* to forgive, she said. So I said, "Okay, Lord, I'm willing to forgive him because You require it of me." Once the willingness is there, God has an open invitation to move in incredible ways.

It helped when I went to the Word and looked at the example Jesus set for us. He was wounded, bruised, and rejected—just as you, the divorced woman, are. But look at the great part: By His stripes (that's the scars from the pain and suffering He endured), *we are healed* (see 1 Peter 2:24)!

When I saw the movie *The Passion of the Christ*, it all came into focus. Seeing this illustration really hit home for me. Here was the battered Christ on the cross, and He said, "Father, forgive them, for they know not what they do." He asked forgiveness *for His own murderers*. That single example is love and forgiveness beyond compare—beyond human comprehension.

He has called us to do the same and gone even further by telling us that He won't forgive us if we don't forgive those who sin against us. Whew! That's a tall order for this hardheaded Italian woman who feels every emotion so deeply that sometimes it's crippling. We are made of flesh and blood. We are human beings, not a sinless, perfect God-man like Jesus. I said, "Why, God, have you asked me to do the impossible?" He told me nothing was impossible with Him. Philippians 4:13 spells it out plainly: "I can do *all things* through Christ who strengthens me" (NKJV, italics mine).

I guess that's the key to conquering our feelings of unforgiveness. We must walk in the spirit and not in the flesh. The battle between the spirit and the flesh is huge. We must pray for more of Him and less of us. For it's not by might, not by power, but only by His Spirit that we can achieve this monumental task (see Zech. 4:6).

We don't want to forgive Fred because we don't think he deserves it. (Instead, we wanted to hit him over the head with the pasta maker). But do *we* deserve forgiveness from God? Did His murderers deserve forgiveness that day?

Once we know we have to forgive our Freds in order to

CONNIE'S LIFE LESSONS
The Acceptance Stage

Remember that when Jesus rose from the dead, His wounds may have healed, but He still had the scars on His hands and His feet. Over time, we will heal, too, but we will also bear scars. When the roots of anger and bitterness are plucked from your wounds, they will finally close up and become scars. Learn to embrace the scars, for each scar has brought you into a deeper and closer walk with the Savior.

be obedient to God, how in the world do we do it? The only way it works for me is to die to myself daily and give all of my emotions—the feelings of anger, bitterness, hatred, betrayal, and rejection—to Him. Remember, He has been there. He felt just as we do. Just think about that for a moment. Honestly say, "God, You know how I feel and I can't do this alone. I need divine intervention here." Your willingness and faith in God will give you the wherewithal to accomplish what He has called you to do.

You're really doing it for yourself. It's your key to freedom. If you don't forgive him, you'll be behind bars the rest of your life carrying the heavy weight of bitterness. You've already lost enough. Don't lose God's blessing for your life because your heart is too hardened to hear Him.

I once knew a woman who was so angry at her father that she had become severely bitter. That woman became ill, and her illness eventually caused her death. I don't know if harboring that hatred and unforgiveness caused her to be sick, but I know that it can cause stress to the point of physical illness. So forgive your former husband for the Lord's sake—and for your own. You don't have to make an appointment with him or write him a letter and tell him. You don't have to be friends or even have a relationship with him other than as a coparent or casual acquaintance. Just forgive him in your own heart of hearts and before God, and remember to pray for him.

I recall an evening before our divorce was final when we were dividing our personal assets into piles on the floor in the house we were about to move out of—our dream house with the lovely garden I labored over. I sat at the kitchen table with him afterward and told him how sorry I was for whatever I did that made him feel our marriage was so hopeless that it wasn't even worth trying to save. I apologized to him and asked him to forgive me. He accepted my apology. I waited for him to apologize to me and ask for my forgiveness for not trying to save us and for choosing another woman over me. He didn't. I was so disappointed. It was only later that I realized that my forgiving is not contingent upon his response.

When you forgive, don't expect anything in return. But forgive all the same. Someday, God will say to you, "Well done, my good and faithful servant."

Carla

"Forgive Seventy Times Seven?"

When I was a little girl, my sister and I would always dread when our mother introduced herself. From schoolteachers to complete strangers at the grocery store, she would proudly say, "I am "Mrs. Smith, a divorced mother of two children who have a non-supporting father of however-many years." This kind of statement can leave quite an impression on others and on little ears. As a child, I was humiliated. She may as well have said, "I'm a victim; their father is a deadbeat. I'm never going to remarry because men are scum. That's my life story in three seconds. How about you?"

I didn't truly understand my mom and this "label" she wore so proudly until I, too, was a divorced mom of two. I guess you might say that my road to forgiveness began here.

I was so determined that this one event in my life would not define the children and me. I knew that I simply *had* to forgive—to move past it and start anew. Because I had seen up close and personal what happens when you don't. And it wasn't pretty. Of course, this was much easier said than done. Mostly because there were and are so many to forgive. For me, like Michelle and Connie have expressed, it still continues to be an ongoing battle as old hurts are dredged up and new ones appear. As a Christian, you can chant the verse about forgiving "seventy times seven" until you are blue in the face, but only God can give you the strength and courage to help you forgive the unforgivable.

One Sunday afternoon, my precious baby boy (who wasn't exactly a baby anymore at seven years old) asked me, "What is grace?" I had never truly given it a lot of thought. I just took it for granted that grace was a "God thing," something He extended to us even though we are all sinners, and a word found in some of my favorite hymns. Before I knew it, I blurted out my answer, "Grace is when you forgive someone who doesn't deserve it." He seemed satisfied and bounced out of the room to conquer yet another pirate with his toy sword, leaving me to ponder. I realized that my path to forgiving had been marked by roadblocks because I either didn't think someone deserved forgiving or they hadn't asked for it.

Suddenly, I understood that in the eyes of grace, neither condition holds up. God's Word tells us that we cannot expect God to forgive us until we have forgiven others. It doesn't say anything about "if" they deserve it or "after" you make them wait ten years. My preacher told us one Sunday that someone once said, "Bitterness is like a cup of poison that *you* drink, but you expect the other person to die."

My mom was like this. She never truly forgave my dad, and she despised my stepmother. Walking in her shoes during my own divorce helped me to finally understand her bitterness. It gave me a whole new perspective and helped me to gradually allow myself to forgive her for wounding me and making me feel so horrible as a child.

In the situation with my former husband, one way that I tried to rise above and at least "fake it until I felt it" was to refer to him as "the children's father." I also called their visitation "parenting time" or "time with Dad." During my divorced parent's class, mandated by the court in my state, they noted that this would be helpful, since the words "ex" and "visitation" were typically associated with prisoners and jails. I never wanted my sweet children to feel like their lives were parallel to Death Row. Since I was a parent, I was forced to be an adult and find a way to be gracious.

Gracious was something I could do. After all, I was a southern gal, a "Georgia Peach," if you will, and being gracious was something we were supposed to be born with, right? I can honestly say that on occasion I was the epitome of a gracious southern belle, but there were also times when my lacy hoop petticoat and parasol were nowhere to be found. I had to work daily at forgiving him, her, myself . . . and even God. Yep, my anger and bitterness extended all the way to heaven. Many a night I lay awake crying and asking God, "Why?" Why had He let this happen to me and my babies? Only with my counselor's help did I realize that I will not always know the "why," but I can rest assured that my Savior loves me and that He will indeed help me through this time.

Ironically, even though at times I was angry with Him, too, it was through God that I finally found a way to forgive myself. During the denial stage, I constantly thought, *What if I had been different?* I thought of all the hateful things I had said to my husband during our marriage. Old hurts ran the gamut from being left alone in the hospital trying to pass a kidney stone when I was pregnant with our son to the times when our baby daughter screamed when she saw him because she didn't recognize him (He had been home for such short periods between trips). I simply had to find a way to forgive myself for the "scare" tactics I had used in my marriage and the old resentment. I even admitted the times that I had yelled and cursed and swore that I hated him. I had actually challenged him to find some flight attendant and cheat on me so we could get it over with. That was the toughest one for me to forgive, since that's the way it actually ended up happening.

The ultimate southern belle test came for me years later, after my divorce and after I had remarried. It was one of the most difficult days of my life. My husband and I had just returned home from the hospital. We never thought that we could have a child due to my endometriosis, but we had conceived only to lose the baby ten weeks later. My visit to the hospital was for surgery after a miscarriage.

The plan was for the children's father to bring them home later that afternoon. I didn't want to involve him in such a private matter, but I felt I should tell him about our loss so he would be prepared if something dreadful happened while I was under anesthesia. All he could say was, "I didn't know you were trying." Then, realizing how he sounded, he simply said that it was none of his business.

What happened next still seems completely unbelievable, yet God must have known that I would need to be spaced out on painkillers to endure "the meeting." Yes, after nearly three years, on the very day when my heart was in a thousand pieces and my self-esteem was at an all-time low (feeling that somehow the loss of our child was my fault), that was the day that my former husband chose to bring "her" to my house. Maybe he thought she would just sit in the truck, and I would be inside the house. But no, my cherubs burst through the door because they couldn't wait for Mommy to meet Daddy's friend. The friend that they had talked about and known on and off for years, but who had never met their Mom before.

I was absolutely flabbergasted (but thankfully still drugged). Then I saw my kids' shining eyes, joyous with excitement and pleading with my own. My mind drifted back to all of the times that I had wanted to share good stuff with my mom about visits to my dad's house and how my stepmom had made these really cool cupcakes out of ice cream cones or how she used to let us dress Muffy the cat up in baby doll clothes—and how my mother wouldn't hear it. I couldn't do that to my own children. Somehow I would have to gather myself together. This was important for the kids.

I didn't even need to look in the mirror. I had on no makeup, and my eyes were bloodshot from tears. My hair was frizzy and ridiculous looking from a recent perm. I knew I had to do this. It was not about me; it was about the children. I knew that somehow God would get me through it.

It was a short exchange. As she stepped from the truck, I saw a beautiful lady, slim and trim, with the most amazing eyes. Her hair was the same shade as my daughter's. As she was introduced to us, I simply shook her hand and said, "The children speak very highly of you." That was it. No more, no less.

I would love to be able to tell you that as they drove away, I never thought of it again. But I cannot. I wallowed for days in the depression of not only losing my baby but also feeling like I had lost my other children to this woman who had been involved in the break-up of my marriage.

Was our divorce her fault? No, it took years and years for

CARLA'S LIFE LESSONS
The Acceptance Stage

True forgiveness means not disparaging your children's dad. Your children are still his children, too. The best thing you can do for your kids is love their parent. Kids are smart enough to even pick up on tone. Try to say "Dad" or "Daddy," if that's what you used to say to them. Switching to "Father" indicates a formality that can make them uncomfortable. Maybe you are uncomfortable and formal with him, but they should not have to be. That is a huge order for you, yes, but it gives your kids permission to relax, to let go of loyalty conflicts, to quit worrying about making somebody mad, and to get on with the business of being kids.

our marriage to break down so much that the only way he could find was a way out. Do I think that if she had not been in the picture, then we could have worked through it? Maybe, maybe not. What I do know is that God has helped me realize that for everything that happens in my life, I can only control *my* attitude and how *I* act. I could choose to be bitter and unforgiving and pass the cup of poison onto my children, or I could choose to take it day-by-day, choice-by-choice, taking the high road as much as possible.

Don't get me wrong; I am not perfect. There are times when I have to apologize to my children and to others, but hopefully with God's grace I will stay on the right road and the detours will be minimal. There will be Little League games and graduations, marriages and grandchildren, many occasions to practice my best southern-belle, Georgia-peach routine. Anyone seen my parasol?

Rosalind

"Why Should I Forgive?"

Once reality hit and my divorce was final, I realized I, too, still had to go through another process—the painful process of forgiveness. This process was truly the most difficult because it was something I did not want to do. I had to find a way to forgive two individuals who had hurt and betrayed me like no one ever had done before. I, too, asked the Lord,

"Why? Why do I have to forgive them? They are the ones who hurt me."

When I reflected on the feelings I had in my heart, forgiveness was so far from what I was feeling. You see, I really struggled with this whole forgiveness thing. I was in tremendous pain, yet somehow I was supposed to find a way to forgive the one who'd caused me the pain in the first place. I could not find a way to get past that pain to forgive anyone. It was not just my former husband or his new love that I needed to forgive, but also others. In my case, I really felt like some of the ministry leaders and church members who were close to me had let me down, too. At one of my greatest times of need, when I was searching for help, the people I expected to be there for me were nowhere to be found.

What was I to do? I felt like my son and I were ignored and neglected. Because of the way I felt, I began a search for a new place of worship. I needed a church family who would provide me with the love and support I needed. A church that had the resources and assistance that would get me through during this difficult time of my life. I needed help, and I needed it desperately.

Sisters, if you are facing a situation similar to mine, please do not respond emotionally without forethought. Instead seek God and ask Him what you should do. Consult with the pastor and let him know what you are going through and what you need. God is looking out for you, and He will make sure you get through. I thank God I ended up at a church that had everything I needed. However, I left the other church without consulting God and the pastor. I allowed my emotions to lead me rather than seeking God's will.

Despite what I had done, God still worked it all out for my good. At the new church I participated in a divorce recovery group, which is when the forgiveness issue really hit home for me.

When we had our discussion and homework assignment on forgiveness, I realized I had no other choice but to endure this difficult process. There was one particular Scripture that really hit me like a ton of bricks. It was convicting; it made me acknowledge my stubborn and unwilling heart. The verse was Matthew 6:14-15: "For if you forgive men when they sin against you, your heavenly Father will also forgive you. But if you do not forgive men their sins, your Father will not forgive your sins" (NIV). After reading those verses, along with others, I prayed to the Lord asking Him to help me because I knew I could not do it alone. Yes, I had a choice; I could hold onto the unforgiveness. But I realized the unforgiveness was only going to destroy my life, not their lives.

After my divorce, I really began to seek God on a more intimate level and I had a desire to study and learn more about His word. Being at this new church gave me an opportunity to get plugged in so I immediately signed up for a small-group Bible study. The group leader contacted me right away. During our conversation, I was shocked to learn they would be doing a study on forgiveness. I immediately started crying on the phone because I knew this was an answer to my prayer for God to help me to take steps toward acceptance. He knew what I needed and provided it right when I needed it. I stayed in that group for more than a year and learned so much. There were several ladies in the group who had also experienced the tremendous pain of divorce. They were such a huge support for me.

Once I was finally able to forgive I was able to walk forward and begin to see the light at the end of the tunnel. God showed me I was not the victim; I was a child of the Most High and I was victorious. He has taught me and continues to teach me how to forgive. So I encourage you, sisters, to keep moving forward. Don't hold onto bitterness or resentment. Find Scriptures on forgiveness and meditate on them day and night. God has a future for you that is be-

ROSALIND'S LIFE LESSONS
The Acceptance Stage

Divorce recovery groups can be a lifeline. I can't recall how I heard about the divorce recovery group at my church, but this wonderful group of people was such a support and played an important part in my healing process. Being in the group really helped me to face the issues I was dealing with and transition from being married to being divorced. I encourage you to seek out such a group. You might not think you need it, but once there you will realize how much you've been trying to shoulder on your own. Give yourself the freedom of accepting their support and encouragement during this difficult phase.

Forgiving Yourself, Forgiving Him, Forgiving Others

Write a letter to your former husband letting him know you forgive him. Include a list of everything you are angry about with him, everything you may hate him for, everything you wish he would have done differently. At the end of the letter, write this phrase: "I forgive you for what I feel you did to me." Repeat this phrase twenty times.

Fold the letter, or place it in an envelope. Do not send the letter, because this letter is for you (and because it can be used against you in court!). Put it into a box. Kneel with that box, and ask God for the strength to forgive. Ask Him to assist you because you cannot forgive without His help.

Pray a prayer that goes something like this:

Lord, in my strength I cannot forgive. So I ask You to give me the will to forgive. Help me to see my former husband as You see him. Help this hate, anger, bitterness, and unforgiveness to leave my heart. Help me to be free of all the bad memories, the ugly words, the many disappointments, and unmet ex-

yond anything you can imagine for yourselves. He wants the very best for you. So focus on what you contribute to the situation, then give it to God. John 8:36 says, "If the Son sets you free, you will be free indeed" (NIV). Rejoice and walk in your freedom!

pectations I received from my former husband. Lord, help me to look at myself, my own humanity, my own failures, the way I have disappointed You, failed You, and turned away from Your promises. Most important, help me to see how You have forgiven me, loved me, and unconditionally cared for me. Help me to have Your heart in this situation and to cling to Your Word for the freedom I long for. Forgive me, Lord, for the wrongs I committed against my husband, the disappointments I brought to him, and the unmet expectations he experienced. Bless him and give him the same new start you have granted me. In Jesus' name, Amen.

This may be difficult for you to pray, but keep trying as you move through this process of forgiveness. As you say it over and over, it will become real for you if your heart is open to change.

Once you've gotten through this initial stage of anger, put the letter box away and only read it during those times when you find yourself struggling with anger again. When you finally reach the point where you know you've fully released your anger to God—when you know it's a genuine release and not wishful thinking on your part—bury the box.

Final Thoughts

Acceptance is a step toward God and a step away from your past. Freedom is found in forgiveness. We want you to be free from your anger, free from your bitterness and resentment, so that you can be free to move on. It is a choice each one of us had to make, and it is one we continue to make daily. Each of us is in a different stop along the path. We freely admit that we have not completely overcome and conquered in this area. So you know that we walk in your shoes and fully understand what we are asking you to do.

We are reminding ourselves, as we are telling you, that forgiveness is a process. It is extremely difficult and is not an overnight thing. Each one of us is faced with the choice to forgive, but really it is the only healthy choice you can make. Aren't you sick and tired of being sick and tired? Don't you get so weary of hating? Lay it down daily. Ask God to pick up that heavy burden and cast it into the sea. Don't give up on acceptance. Don't feel discouraged if you don't feel like you can forgive. It will come if you are willing to keep at it as a desire and a goal. Our anger didn't happen overnight and neither will our letting go of it. Remember, a decision to forgive and trust again is a decision to live, laugh, and love again.

We will live.
We will laugh,
And, yes, we will love again!

Five Action Points on the Road Toward Forgiveness and Acceptance

1. Let go! You have to come to terms with the reality that you may never see justice here on this Earth. In order to forgive you have to let go of the need for justice. We've heard many people say, "Yeah, I can forgive, but I won't forget." Sorry. No such thing. If you dwell on every little thing he ever did to you, you will never forgive him. Dwelling on those memories only puts us right back there again, and every old feeling it produced in us comes out as a result.

2. Take the "litmus test" of healing. You will know you have truly forgiven and been healed from your old hurts if you can look back at the most painful events and scenes in your marriage and divorce and feel no pain attached to them! It happens, trust us! When the forgiveness and acceptance process is complete, looking back at your old life will be like watching an old movie. Your mind will know that you actually lived all that stuff, but your heart won't feel it. It will be just like it happened to somebody else. Can we hear an "Amen" to that?

3. Keep up the good work. One time of forgiving isn't enough, nor is two or five or twenty-five. Jesus said we must forgive "seventy times seven" times, but don't take that number literally. You may have counted way beyond 490 times that he trampled your heart, but

don't stop there. Jesus meant that you should keep on keepin' on . . . until He returns to take you home.

4. Don't confuse forgiveness with friendship. We are not asking you to be best buddies with your former husband and his new love. Establish clear and proper boundaries so that the chance for conflict and confusion is eliminated.

5. Do not buy the lie that your life has ended because the divorce is final. In a way, it is just beginning. You may not have chosen for the road to split this way, but the Lord will take you to some beautiful new stops on your life's journey.

Survival Checklist

✳ *Pray*—Prayer, prayer, and more prayer is the only thing that will help you to forgive.

✳ *Counsel*—We can't stress enough the importance of having a neutral party to listen to you vent and give you wisdom. See a counselor who can help you talk through all the pain and hurt you have bottled up inside of you.

✳ *Friends*—When you're having difficulty accepting or forgiving, call a friend who can help hold you accountable and help you to let go of your feelings.

✳ *Respect*—Practice ways in which to show respect and kindness to the father of your children (without crossing boundaries). For example, instead of accidentally forgetting to pack the kids' shoes so he has to buy some, you not only pack their shoes, but you also organize everything to make it easier for him. Instead of refusing to compromise on visitation, work with him to make the changes he needs.

 * *Thoughts*—Every time the thoughts of anger, hate, or resentment for your former spouse even enter your mind, put them out. Don't even entertain them, because they fuel your feelings and act themselves out in other ways in your life.

Chapter 6

You Are Not Alone–Testimonies from Those Who've Been There

"And surely I am with you always, to the very end of the age."
—*Matthew 28:20 NIV*

Now that we have walked through the stages of grief we experience during divorce, we'd like to reassure you that we are not the only ones to feel this pain. Neither are you. Rich or poor, regular Jane or famous movie star, no one is immune to the ravages of divorce. Instead of throwing more statistics at you, let's look at some examples in real life.

For instance, imagine being someone like actress Nicole Kidman and having to go through a divorce publicly. She had to shield her children from the tabloids as they made claims that her husband, actor Tom Cruise, was having an affair.

Later, we cheered when Nicole was interviewed on a late-night talk show and, when asked about life after Tom, said that she could now wear heels again. She was much taller than Tom and had for years worn flats to make him feel better. Now she could be herself again.

Half of all American children today will grow up in a single-parent home sometime during their childhood or adolescence, according to Dr. Richard Land in *Real Homeland Security: The America God Will Bless*.[4] All you have to do is look at your child's class roster and see how the children's last names are different from their mothers'. This is not the day of June and Ward Cleaver, and that's sad. It's sad for our nation, sad for ourselves, and sad for our children. All the statistics and stories show you that you are not alone. There are broken hearts and wounded women everywhere. Some are healing and moving on; some are still stuck and scheming to get their former spouse.

We talked to many other women who have endured a divorce or even two. We asked some of them to share when they felt most alone and what advice they have for surviving. Here are our stories and theirs:

Carla

I will never forget the day I walked out of his attorney's office after signing "the papers." It was the most alone I had ever felt.

It was a blur, really. I was crying so much that my contacts fell out of my eyes, and my windows to the world looked like someone had spread Vaseline on the glass. I do remember the faces of the ladies in the offices of Dewey, Cheatham & Howe. (Not a real firm, of course, but did we make you laugh?) They stared at me with a pity I thought should be reserved for people with terminal illnesses. As I sat there looking at the pile of papers that officially dissolved my family and life as I had known it, I wondered why I didn't feel more relief.

After all the lawyer stuff and the haggling over DVDs and Grandma's quilt, I think I felt disappointed. At what, I'm not sure—that I didn't get my day in court? That no one official heard "my side of the story"? Maybe I was disappointed that my husband didn't come running through the door, beg for my forgiveness, and ask me to try again. A mixture of bitterness, regret, and an overwhelming sense of being alone filled my heart. It was an odd ending to a relationship that had begun with such fanfare at the wedding. Where were all the family and friends? The champagne? The cake? This was when I needed people the most, and some comfort food might've come in handy during this horrendous time. Isn't it ironic? Newlyweds could care less who's even in the room and can't wait to be alone. At the other end of the marital spectrum is the divorcee who could really use at least one of those smiling faces from the reception so she *wouldn't* have to be alone.

I vote that we start a new tradition—in addition to holding the ring and making a toast at the reception, the best man must accompany the bride-to-be-no-more if she ever has to sign divorce papers. What do you think?

All kidding aside, you will encounter many alone times—times when you'll feel like you're the only person on the face of the earth. Perhaps it'll be when you take your child to the doctor and the nurse calls out "Mrs. Smith?" And your mind will be screaming "I'm not a Mrs.! I'm a Ms.!" Or maybe it will be the first holiday, and it'll take you by surprise. I recall the first Father's Day—just a month since he'd dropped the bomb and I was still in denial. I stood in the choir balcony singing my little heart out. And right after that the preacher started talking about—what else?—being a father. My eyes welled up, and I began to sniffle. I was an idiot for thinking I could sit up there in the loft right behind the preacher as the fathers all came forward and then the wives and children followed to lay hands on their husbands' and daddies' backs to pray for them. I began to sob uncontrollably and had to leave the loft. I praise God for people like the pastor's wife and her daughter, who drove the children and me home that day.

You must know in those times God will intercede on your behalf. He is the Father to the fatherless and the Husband who will never leave you. You absolutely must claim that God will never forsake you, nor leave you (see Deut. 31). There is a wonderful song by Point of Grace—"You Will Never Walk Alone." Listen to it. Meditate on it. Remember that you have an entire family of girlfriends to hear your cries and feel your pain with you. Including us!

Rosalind

When my son had his first visit with his dad the summer after the divorce, I really felt alone. His dad lives out of state, and it was very difficult to let my child go. I was dreading this visit because I knew I would be alone, and mentally and emotionally, I was not prepared. While packing my son's clothes, I thought to myself, *Why do I have to endure this? Why do I have to be separated from my son? Who will I take care of? Oh, the quietness of the house is going to drive me insane. I will not hear my little boy playing with his toys or running through the house saying, "Mama, Mama, I am hungry. Mama, I am sleepy. Mama, I am thirsty." Lord, what am I going to do?*

During the time he was away, I could not sleep and felt so afraid of being in the house alone. Every noise was magnified and kept me restless. It was so strange to go from a house filled with laughter and family routine to a life alone and filled with fear. My son was temporarily gone from me, and I was forced to find a way to survive those lonely nights and to face my fears knowing God would protect me.

What I learned through that hard time was that it really is okay to be alone. The time allowed me to care for myself and rejuvenate my mind, body, and spirit. Sisters, you will experience loneliness and the fear that goes with being alone. However, seize this as an opportunity to take time for you. Go to the movies, hang out with friends, put in a workout tape, or go to the gym. Take yourself out to eat. Live life.

Another way to overcome the loneliness is to open the

Word of God and let it minister to your soul. Cry out to God and share what you are feeling because He already knows. Spending that alone time with Him will comfort your soul. Surrender this time, and let Him fill you.

There have been times, even in the midst of my busy schedule, even when I was walking with the Lord, when real loneliness occurred. Loneliness can come most unexpectedly, even when we think we are finally past it all. While handling the daily routine, those feelings of loneliness will creep in again. That's when you have to cling to the promise that what you're feeling is a lie. You are never truly alone. God is with you, and He is there to walk through your darkest moments. When you feel lonely, call out to Him. Then call a friend, someone to whom you are accountable (not those male friends)—and allow her to help you get through this. Alone time can and *will* benefit you if you allow it to. God will always be there; He will never leave you nor forsake you (see Heb. 13:5). Life is too short to put it on hold, so get out there and live it!

Connie

When my daughter got married, she relocated to the town in which her new husband was born and raised. She had lived away from home since the divorce, but when she moved that far away . . . well, it took the "missing" her to a whole new level. Her in-laws decided to give them a reception in their hometown a month after the actual wedding. I was invited to attend. So were Fred and Wilma.

It seemed as though I had been thrown into every painful situation imaginable since my divorce, but this one by far stood out in my mind as the worst. When I showed up at the airport to take the four-and-a-half-hour flight out, there were Fred and Wilma boarding the same plane and sitting two rows in front of me! When we arrived, there they were at the baggage claim where my brother picked me up. When Wilma saw him, she gave him this big hug like he was *her* brother—and she had only just met him the month before. Looking back, I understand it's within her and my brother's rights to have a friendship, but at the time it really hurt.

The entire weekend, I felt sorry for my daughter because she had to split her time between her father and me. On the day of the reception, I was much less busy than the day of the actual wedding because I had not planned this event, and I didn't know any of the invited guests. Therefore, I was all too aware of everything that was going on. Unfortunately, my brother and his wife could not attend, so I was alone. I was meeting all the guests alone and had plenty of time to see Fred and Wilma together. There were times during the three-hour event that I wasn't speaking with anyone and just stood there by myself. I felt like every eye was on me. I felt as if there was this big "D" on my dress. I made small talk with Fred, but I found it very difficult to make eye contact with Wilma or even speak to her. If you can believe it, I actually felt bad about not speaking to her because normally, I'm a very social and gracious person. God dealt with me about the way I acted that day. I certainly wouldn't have won a prize for the "What Would Jesus Do?" contest.

One of the most difficult moments was when Wilma said she wanted to go outside and shoot some photos with my daughter and her husband. As the four of them filed out, I was left standing there alone. I have never felt as isolated as I did at that moment, as Wilma mingled with all of the guests, talking about my two daughters as if they were her own. My poor daughter kept watching me to see if I was mingling. If I wasn't, she'd come over right away to rescue me.

All of the anger I thought I had dealt with rose up in me again. I thought I had gotten past this phase! That day showed me once again that forgiveness may be a process that is ongoing the rest of my life. But I will persevere, because God forgives me.

I know I got through it because of the prayer warriors who were lifting me up and because of the truth in God's Word assuring me that "Your Creator will be your husband. The Lord of Hosts is his name; he is your Redeemer" (see Isa. 54:5). I now realize I will *never* be alone again!

Michelle

I knew what lonely meant, and I knew how it felt, but aloneness was something I had actually never really experienced before my divorce. I am the oldest of five kids. At the time of my divorce I had four children, so most of my adult life has been full. There hasn't been a whole lot of time for aloneness. Yet when we separated, and I moved into my new home with my four children, there was no one—*no one*—who could fill this emptiness inside me. I could have been standing in a room full of a thousand people, and I would have felt as if I was in a different world, in a bubble unable to be reached, on another planet, in another universe, completely, utterly alone.

Aloneness for me wasn't where I was or what I was doing or even who I was with; it was my state of mind. I have never felt as alone in my life as I did during my separation and divorce. Evenings only magnified the feeling and left me anxious and more depressed. During the day I could fill my life by going through the motions of my responsibilities as a mother and, now, a provider for my kids. When the evening came, when the kids were in bed, and the lights were out, I felt as if the walls were caving in around me, and I was suffocating from the pain within my heart. I dreaded the night and would lie awake for hours until finally I would fall asleep from pure exhaustion. My kids were late for school most days, and life just seemed a mess. But it was their little faces and my determination to push through, and of course my faith in God, that got me through that time.

Slowly, over time, I began to realize I certainly was not alone. The Lord brought people to me to remind me He in fact had not left me and had not abandoned me. It was very obvious to me that even though I felt alone, even though I hid out because I felt ashamed of what I was going through, my Lord was pursuing me. He sent people into my life to encourage me, to love me, and in the times I felt He wasn't there, He *was*—loving me continuously.

Do you remember the old children's Christmas classic *Santa Claus Is Coming to Town*? It was one of my favorite shows at Christmastime. Do you remember the lyrics, "Put one foot in front of the other, and soon you'll be walking out the door"? Well, that was me. I put one foot on the floor and then eventually the other one, and then slowly I was able to take a step, and then another, until finally I was walking. And yes, eventually I was able to run again. I don't know if I'll ever run the same, but hey, at least I'm running!

There is no formula for healing. Each person is different, and each person will heal in their own time. Be patient with yourself and just know this is a season and it too shall pass. You may feel alone right now. My heart goes out to you. I cannot be there with you, but Jesus can. I cannot hold you in your pain, but He can. Reach out to Him and ask Him to strengthen you, so you will be able to put that first foot on the ground. He will help you walk again, and eventually you will run. But for now, hobble into His arms and let Him comfort you.

Beth[*]

The time I felt the most alone was when I was in the process of divorcing my husband of sixteen years. I initiated the divorce but always had secret doubts about whether it was the right thing. One day in particular stands out in my mind. On that day, I drove three hours to where my husband lived to collect a few more items I felt I wanted before the deed was done. He quietly watched as I loaded the car, and I could feel the pain coming off of him. I watched him in my rearview mirror as I drove away. He just stood there forlornly and watched me leave, and I had horrible feelings of sadness and guilt. I could almost hear him—hear his heart crying out to me: "Please turn the car around; please don't do this."

I drove the three hours home through floods of tears. The farther I drove away, the more devastated I felt, and the harder I cried. I knew in my heart of hearts it was a mistake. I knew I was hurting him horribly. The truth is that I desperately wanted him to come after me, pull me out of the car, tell me he couldn't bear the idea of losing me, and beg me to please come back. But he didn't. I never felt so alone as I did at that moment, driving away into a new life that I could not see mapped out safely ahead of me. I had left behind a man I still loved, but I was hurt and angry and not able or willing to stay to try to work it through anymore.

[*] Names have been changed here and throughout this chapter.

I honestly don't know how I got through those next few hours. I cried so hard I could barely drive. I *knew* I was wrong and that I should turn the car around and go make it right. But at the time I had not yet worked through my anger and hurt, and I kept my foot on the gas.

In the following days I absolutely withered. I lost weight, lost sleep, and felt that horrible heaviness. I didn't go to the Lord out of my own guilt. I think I just purged emotion through crying. As the days passed some of that feeling of being sick passed, too. So I tried coping alone. But as time went on, I found myself going back to the Lord and laying it all before Him, asking Him for help again.

And that's when the healing finally started to come. While I'm still not fully over the trauma, I'm healthy, and my relationship with the Lord is restored. He never left me of course. I left Him and walked alone for awhile. I never intend to do that again.

Jane

After my husband declared we were getting a divorce, I had a very good friend who had been through the same situation who helped me heal in a very healthy way. He was a pastor who had been divorced, and we had worked together in a previous church. I was the pastor's secretary, and he was an associate of the pastor.

Since I had no children and no living relatives, this man,

who was like a brother, and I began to spend time together. He has a degree in counseling and worked on helping me regain my sense of self-worth.

My husband and I had split in May, and in December the church my friend attended—and where I had formerly attended—was having a singles' Christmas party. He invited me to go, not as a date, but just to show up. I planned to go and even asked him to pick me up because I don't drive well at night and really didn't feel like showing up alone even though it was for singles.

Well, when the pastor I worked for found out I would be going to the party with my friend, he condemned me. He said I was wrong, going out to an event like that with a single man when legally I was still married. I was so hurt. I remember lying in a fetal position in bed most of the weekend in the newly acquired apartment that I hated. I was totally alone, crying out to God—a God who I felt had abandoned me. It was the most devastating time I can ever remember with the exception of my mother's early death when I was twenty-three. I became physically and emotionally ill over it. I couldn't eat or drink anything that whole day and night of the party. The next day I couldn't go to church and listen to my pastor preach.

It took me a long time to forgive him for having that attitude toward me. But I knew I had to. I cried out to the Lord and I persevered. It took time and prayer, but eventually healing did come to our relationship. God is so very good!

Sandy

My divorce struggle wore on for a year because my husband wanted full custody of our three children. In the end, the judge granted him every other weekend for visitation. Since we lived thirty minutes away from each other, we agreed to meet at a local restaurant parking lot somewhere in between.

I'll never forget one particular Friday night as we sat in the parking lot waiting for him to arrive. Perhaps sensing my discomfort with the situation, the kids became anxious about leaving me. My youngest child was only two years old at the time. She was very clingy and insecure and was already crying as her dad pulled up. All three kids began to cry, holding onto me saying, "Mommy! Mommy!" We had to listen to this as the children were transferred from my car to his.

When they finally pulled away, my last image of them was of my youngest, looking out the back window, crying. I could see her mouthing, "Mommy!" There I was standing alone in the parking lot late on a Friday afternoon as their father took away my most precious possessions. On some level I understood that the children needed to spend time with their father (a hard thing to admit in light of the history he and I had), but still, it was so incredibly hard to let them go. I numbly got back into my car, drove back to my apartment, and sobbed for hours.

This kind of desperation was a new feeling for me. As I

sat curled up on the floor that night, I had to continuously remind myself that I was not alone. I also concluded that peace has nothing to do with the absence of pain and loneliness. What I mean is that even though I hurt, I was able to draw on God's strength and peace. I spoke the Word of God and held onto it with everything I had. I created new files in my mind and put Scripture with each one, preparing me to cope with future challenges. It was a mental discipline, and it worked. I spoke the Scripture verses aloud in order to cement them in my heart.

Now, ten years later, my former husband still takes the children every other weekend. And I still discipline myself to stand on the Word of God. And it still works. What a blessing.

Toni

I lost everything in my divorce. I lost a bitter custody battle for my children. I lost the wealth I had worked so hard to build up during our marriage. Even my own family abandoned me. I lost my source of income and couldn't find a new job. As a result the bank had begun foreclosure proceedings on my home and my ex-husband was suing me for back payments on the child support he knew I couldn't pay. I was so overwhelmed with sorrow I felt like I wanted to end my life.

There was one night I struggled particularly with that

thought. Just when I needed it most, a friend *happened* to call. She prayed for me and tried to help me find some peace. Another friend had given me a book called *How to Live Through a Bad Day* by Jack Hayford. It is based on the last seven statements Christ made as He hung on the cross. After I hung up I decided to read for awhile to calm my mind. I *happened* to be on the chapter titled, "Aim Your Hard Questions at God, Not Man." It is based on Christ's cry "My God, my God, why have you forsaken me?" As I read, my eyes welled up with tears and I had a good cry. Through my own suffering I gained a new perspective of what Christ endured for me. I had a fresh understanding of how very much He loves me.

You see, God had loved me enough to use two dear friends to help me that night. He knew my desperation and provided exactly what I needed at that moment. I made it through that awful night, and the next one, and the next one. And though things are still difficult at times, He continues to surround me with more friends whose love is restoring my life. I now have hope that brighter days are ahead.

Debra

It was Christmas night. My husband had been on the road with his work for four months. We were spending our seventeenth Christmas together. I was ecstatic! I noticed,

Alone-Time Strategy

Make plans with a girlfriend at least once a week to have dinner, take a walk, and sound off a little. You must find a way to fill your days and plan for those "alone times." Some constructive venting can't hurt, either. What happens when a balloon is filled with too much air? It pops, right? Well, imagine that you are that balloon and you are being filled with a lot of "hot air." You must let some of it out before you pop! Plus, being a friend is important, too. It gets you out of focusing only on yourself (a natural response to divorce) and keeps you looking outward. Make sure you ask your friend how she is doing. Keep your friendship in give-and-take mode, and you'll feel better about yourself.

though, that he was acting strangely. I had no idea how strange that evening would become.

He just came out and said it: "Debra, I don't love you. I never have. Now that I've reached this level of my career, I don't need you anymore."

I sat there stunned at what I had just heard. I felt like I was in a movie. I *was* the movie! All I could do was mutter to myself, "Lord, protect my heart. Protect my heart."

My mind was racing. At forty-five years of age and after seventeen years of marriage, how was I going to cope? *I'll be alone,* I thought. *How will I carry the financial burden of supporting myself and my father* (who was in a retirement center) *and my mother* (who was in a nursing home)? *How will I continue to live?*

"God, are You there?" I asked. "Have You forgotten me? Do You realize how hurt I am? How do I breathe? How could You have allowed this to happen? I worshipped You and I've served You. What is happening here?"

Suddenly a "peace that passes all understanding" (Phil. 4:7) washed over me like a flood, and I knew I would be able to deal with this surreal situation. Somehow I would come out on the other side. I was so thankful to have that confirmation, as I sat there with my husband and realized my marriage was over.

In the days that followed I continued to lean on those feelings. I was able to keep the mind of Christ because my thoughts were established in Him. He directed my steps. It's been five years now. I'm remarried, to the most wonderful man God could have chosen for me. What a miracle He has given me. He truly is faithful.

Cheryl

I remember lying awake the entire night before my legal separation hearing. I honestly felt like God had abandoned me. I have never experienced such darkness, sadness, and overwhelming grief as I felt during that time.

Earlier, my attorney had informed me that my husband

had prepared a false testimony about me in order to keep from having to pay temporary alimony until a settlement could be reached. My heart had been broken to learn that my husband was in a serious relationship with another—a relationship he'd had for the past two years. Now I was devastated to think that the man I loved more than life itself would go so far as to fabricate a vicious lie about me to protect the little amount of money the court was requiring of him.

A friend I had called earlier for prayer contacted my pastor, and he and his wife called from out of town to speak with me and pray for me. But the comfort I experienced through their words evaporated as soon as I hung up the phone. I could truly say this was the lowest point I'd ever experienced. All I could do that night was pace the floor and cry. Through agonizing sobs I could barely utter the name of Jesus. I kept my Bible open and struggled to read and receive any thread of comfort and hope.

Toward sunrise, exhausted and fatigued, I cried out loud, "God, are *You* not with me?" I was stunned to hear in my spirit, *Did I not say to you that if you would believe you would see the glory of God?* I recognized this instantly as Jesus' words just before He called Lazarus forth from the tomb (see John 11:40). Suddenly, hope exploded in my heart. My body felt like electricity had gone through it. I became hopeful. Not that the marriage would be saved, but that God was going to bring me through this and that He would turn it all out for good.

I showered and dressed and went with two friends to the

courthouse that morning. I shared with them the words that God had given me. I sang praises all the way to the appointment. When we arrived I was moved to see that my pastor and his wife had flown in to support me. One by one I saw precious friends, faith and prayer mentors, gather on my behalf because they loved and believed in me. I wept. They prayed.

We took our seats in the courtroom awaiting my name on the roster. Imagine my overwhelming surprise when within minutes my attorney came and whispered in my ear, "It's over. You don't have to go through this. He has withdrawn his accusation and has agreed to fulfill his responsibility."

Healing began for me that day. I have learned that there will be times in our lives when we feel totally abandoned and alone. We do not feel God, nor do we perceive Him to be anywhere near or even close when we need Him most. But understand: *He is there!* He will *always* be there, as He has promised us over and over in His Word.

I now minister on an almost daily basis with people who are hurting and I find comfort to extend to them because I have been comforted by the ultimate Comforter.

Final Thoughts

As you can see, even years after the divorce, many still feel wounded. There will be times when you must grit your teeth and smile at the other woman as she dances with your ex-husband at your precious daughter's wedding.

Times when you must maintain the sanity and self-control that keep you from buying a Hummer and running over the man who abused you and your children for years. Times when you must find a way to forgive the man you loved after he walked out on you and your two-year-old child, leaving you penniless. Every new day is a choice, a fresh, clean slate on which to make the most of what God has given you. Here's the deal: surviving divorce is not about going from one phase to another and constantly moving forward like a game of checkers (though you may feel like you are getting jumped from behind all the time). There isn't a winner and a loser. You don't escape future episodes of anger because you have survived the depression and are learning to forgive.

Instead, surviving divorce is more like the children's game Candyland. Each day you draw colorful cards on your way to see King Kandy. Some days you might skip ahead of Lord Licorice and Gramma Nutt to visit Queen Frostine in the Ice Cream Sea. Those days, you think, *Hey, my life's not so bad; I'm doing the forgiving thing and moving on nicely.* Then one day, you get mad at your former husband for changing the parenting time schedule, *again*, and you draw the Gloppy card only to get stuck in Molasses Swamp. You might even sound off one day at the new stepmom during Parent-Teacher night, "Why don't you go and have your own kids and leave mine alone?" Oops, looks like someone drew the purple Plumpy card, and he is pulling you all the way back to the beginning to start all over again!

Although we are loving the Candyland analogy, we must make sure you understand the point: You will travel from phase to phase and at every stop along the path there will be new experiences, some good and some not so good. You will get through them all because you are not alone. You have the Lord. You have friends, family, or kids. And hey, you have all of us, too! So buck up and make an effort every day to keep playing the game. Life is sweet. Ultimately, we will all be sitting in the Candy Castle with the greatest King, eating the most delicious chocolate that has no fat or calories! And meanwhile . . .

We will live.
We will laugh.
And, yes, we will love again!

Five Action Points for Making It Through the Alone Times

1. Find friends, be a friend, stick with your friends. While you may want to stay home curled up in a fetal position, it's not healthy. Don't let your poor self-image convince you that your friends don't want to see you anymore. If your phone isn't ringing, maybe it's because you've been withdrawn for so long. Or maybe they just feel awkward and don't know what to say. Give them a break. Pick up the phone and make a lunch date.

2. Plan for your alone times. Look ahead to the dates

your kids will be gone, and fill in the alone time with chores, house projects, church, meals with friends, and even grocery shopping. Keep yourself moving.

3. Start a journal of your blessings and answers to prayer. Write every little thing you can think of that is positive or a sign of the Lord working in your life. Take it out during your worst alone times (such as the middle of the night) and re-read your entries. Thank the Lord for these blessings.

4. Get plugged in to Christian fellowship. Find a divorce recovery class, a Bible study, a small group, a singles' class, or all of the above (smile). Spend time learning more about your relationship with the Lord and relationships with friends who have faith in common.

5. Get out of your house and try something new—just for you. Take an art class, try gourmet cooking, or train for a marathon. Consider going back to school. Do some of the things you have always wanted to do but never had the time for. You deserve it!

Survival Checklist
The Alone Times

✳ *Friends*—Do not—we repeat, *do not*—go by yourself to sign the papers. If you are like Carla and lose your contacts due to crying (and you will cry), you won't be able to drive anyway. Take a friend along to any major "family" event—weddings, baptisms, graduations—too. You don't have to hire a hunky escort. Take your best girl-friend. She will tell you when your smile has disappeared or if you are getting that dangerous gleam in your eyes. Take a friend or family member with you to any other event—soccer games, dance recitals, Little League. These aren't minor events emotionally, and you must plan ahead.

Sounding Board—Check with one or two best friends and see if they would be willing to be your sounding board, walking with you through your separation, divorce, and recovery. Plan activities with these friends regularly. You need that sounding board as you deal with all of the emotions.

Shopping—If nighttime is your worst time, turn on the TV or hop on the Internet. You can get a head start on your Christmas shopping with all of the infomercials that are on (but stay away from going into debt to do so), and these days you can purchase just about anything online with a credit card and a click of the mouse (eBay is lots of fun!).

Baby-sitter—Start cultivating baby-sitters you trust, as well as taking advantage of the nights when you have free baby-sitting by Dad. When you're ready to date again, plan dates for those nights when the kids will be with Daddy. Take it very slow, though (more on that later).

Pray—Yeah, this one is still on the list. It never goes out of style. Keep praying every day. Talk to God. He knows your heart, but He still wants to hear from you.

✳ *Bible*—Buy a Bible, a fresh one for you to make notes and highlight favorite verses in. If reading is hard for you, consider picking up one of the well-done audio Bibles, available on cassette, CD, or even MP3 files. There are Bibles in magazine format, complete with fun quizzes and Top 10 lists, and there are Bibles with study features, maps, concordances, and multiple translations. Try it; you'll like it!

✳ *Church*—Find a church so you can be supported by other believers. Period. End of story. Not optional. Just do it.

✳ *Music*—Tune in to your local Christian radio station. Music can be a wonderful blessing and help you on your walk with the Lord.

✳ *Favorite Phrase*—Don't forget to keep repeating your favorite phrase: "I will live, I will laugh, and, yes, I will love again!"

Chapter 7

Life After Divorce—The Good, the Bad, and the Ugly

"Yet in all these things we are more than conquerors through Him who loved us."
—*ROMANS 8:37 NKJV*

Well, girls, here we are. Welcome to your new career. You're a . . . plate spinner! A juggler! A mommy! A nurse! A housecleaner! An employee! And much, much more! (And you thought you were doing a lot when you were married.) Well, if all else fails, we can all qualify for careers in the circus.

Now that you are single, the duties you had in your previous life as a married woman are compounded, multiplied. They take on a whole new meaning. Everything may seem to hit you at once—the kids, the bills piling up, the laundry, the house, your job or lack of a job, school, and more. Suddenly, everything is dependent upon you. The whole kit and caboodle (What is a "kit and caboodle," anyway?) Saying it's overwhelming is an understatement. You may have to take a crash course in prioritizing, because you can't do it all. Not now. Not ever. As one friend's father always puts it, "Just do the best you can with what you've got."

Going solo definitely takes some getting used to. You may find yourself going to extremes. Some women totally let themselves go, losing interest in their appearance. Others dress very provocatively in hopes of attracting other men. Just because we're divorced women, that doesn't give us a license to put our brains on the shelf and act like teenagers who have been in an all-girls' school for years. We are so vulnerable now, probably more than ever before in our lives, and we must think with our heads and not just our hearts or our emotions. It's normal to want to be held and touched. However, God's standards are still the same, whether we're single for the first time or single again.

After divorce, we will continue to experience hurts, especially where the children are concerned. We will have feelings of resentment and anger because we have to live with things we never expected to have to live with. Constantly remind yourself that you don't have to get over this in any certain amount of time. It's easy to be too hard on yourself. Give yourself time, and give yourself a break. This is a huge transition to deal with, and there will be ups and downs. Just do the best you can, and remember to take it one day at a time.

See this phase after divorce as an opportunity—a new chapter in your life. Take a long look at yourself. What have you always wanted to do? Where have you always wanted to go? Find ways to make those things happen. Most of all, try to bring balance into your life. Don't let things become too one-sided. All work and no recreation is unhealthy. All for the kids and nothing for yourself isn't good. Neither is forgetting your kids to chase after your latest dream (or man)!

Make a list of your goals and priorities for the day, the year, and five years. Then start working toward them. Put a little cash aside, and get that makeover. Don't neglect the exercise and those counseling sessions you desperately need. You will be amazed at what you're capable of and how far you've come.

Michelle

"Fixing Me Instead of Fixing Him"

Does it get any uglier than divorce? We say things we don't mean, we do things we would normally never do. We feel like crud 24/7, we look like crud 24/7, and, well, we eat crud 24/7. I think the word *loser* would best describe how I felt during that time.

It is inevitable we are going to make mistakes. Even after

you read this book you may go out and do the very things we have warned you not to do. Why? Because from the time our divorce begins we are thrown into a spin that doesn't stop until long after the divorce papers are signed. Do you remember as a kid jumping on the little spinning merry-go-round? It moved so fast jumping off was not an option. I'd come off that thing dizzy and unable to focus on the world around me. I would thrust myself to the ground until I could get my bearings again. I loved that feeling of not knowing where I was and not being able to see clearly until all had settled inside my little body.

Divorce put me in a spin and created in me this immediate insecurity and vulnerability I had never before experienced. I was on a fast merry-go-round and nothing around me was clear. I knew no one who had gone through a divorce. It was so foreign to me. I actually thought I was the only one who had ever experienced the things I was feeling and I was completely unprepared. As a result I didn't get my bearings for a while. I really allowed my thoughts and feelings to control me.

Thankfully, I did finally get help. I think the greatest thing I learned and the good that has come as a result of my divorce is what I have done for myself. Instead of focusing on all of the things he did, I focused on all the things I needed to work on. I sat with my counselor, and the first thing I asked is: "How do I fix me? How do I get rid of this darkness inside my heart, this anger that is eating me alive, this unforgiveness that is stealing my joy, the regret that is keeping me from my tomorrow?" And most important, "How do I get off this dang merry-go-round?"

Okay, of course I made many mistakes. Who goes through life without mistakes? I think the opposite sex was the foremost thing on my mind, including, frankly, sex and the lack of it. I am a very loving, affectionate person, and I had already spent several years cut off from my former husband both emotionally and physically. I knew it was bad when I started checking to see if the garbage man was looking my way.

Here's the deal. Remember the spin. Understand that when you are spinning, well, anyone could look halfway decent. Nothing is in focus—or should I say men are not in focus. You might as well be looking through those 3-D glasses your kids got at the last *Spy Kids* movie. Bottom line? Don't even think about dating or engaging in any conversation with the opposite sex until your divorce is final and you are on your way to a healthy you (let your counselor help you determine when that is).

When I lost my husband—or should I say when he lost me (smile)—I immediately wanted to fix it. I felt like I was bleeding uncontrollably and had to find a way to stop the hemorrhaging. I wanted to find a replacement husband as soon as possible. The thought of being alone was the death sentence to me. After all, I had not been alone in fifteen years. I allowed fear and loneliness to rule my heart. I had to know if someone would still want me. I remember looking at men wondering if they could even see me, if they

MICHELLE'S LIFE LESSONS
The After-Divorce Stage

When your life is spinning like a merry-go-round, you are too dizzy to focus, too out of touch with reality to really see clearly. This is why it is so important to surround yourself with "safe" people. Safe people are those who will love you through the 24/7 crud, who can watch you cry your guts out on their shoulders and be unaffected by your endless runny nose and your uninterrupted chatter of all "he" did to you. These "safe" people are people who love you unconditionally—those who you could trust with a million dollars and the PIN to your bank account.

even took notice when I walked into the room. On the other hand, I was scared to death of the idea of dating again.

I had a few "friends" who would occupy my time and keep me company, but the thought of getting "out there" in the game of life and trying to figure all that out was terrifying. My insecurity was heightened. I mean, I had thought I had good judgment the first time, and look what happened! How would I ever be able to trust myself—let alone any man—again?

It wasn't until I really gave up my fears to the Lord and accepted that my singleness could be forever that God completely, unexpectedly brought me a husband. In fact, when I met my husband I had actually come to terms with the fact that singleness might be beneficial. I would have no one to take care of, no one to answer to, no one to worry about, and, of course, no one to love and possibly lose. I even started wearing a ring on my fourth finger to symbolize my marriage to God. He would be my only lover and friend. God had shown me that He could truly be everything I needed. It was amazing to see for the first time in my life that I actually could stand on my own. It felt good to know I could walk with Him and Him alone.

Only when I was on my way to healing was I able to be okay with or without another marriage.

The simple truth is that no one but God can complete you. Not a man or even your child. It is so difficult when we feel abandoned not to try to fill the void with another person. This is why I stress the importance of talking through these needs with a counselor and, most important, praying and asking God for strength and eyes to be opened to the truth.

Connie

"The 'Get Over It' Clock Is Ticking"

Honestly, girls, since my own divorce I have talked to many women who have gone through or are going through this ride to hell and back. It absolutely breaks my heart to see the way women suffer over it. I talked with a woman who has been divorced for ten years, and she's still not over it. She was married to her husband for thirty-five years. He left her for another woman who was the same age as their daughter. Her attorney was able to get her alimony for the rest of her life. That was a high price for him to pay, but his wife was worth it.

Another woman I know went completely off the deep end and started bar hopping and sleeping with whomever, which is totally contrary to what she truly believes is right. In other words, she temporarily went nuts.

For every woman it's different. Some heal and move on faster than others. There's no right or wrong time limit. Some people will expect you to "get over it" after a certain amount of time has passed. If you've moved on in your job, have good friends, or are even dating again, they will expect you to be fine. They think those other things will fill the void of the lost-marriage hole in your heart. *Wrong!* They don't get it. Nothing fills that gaping hole, that wound from divorce, except wise counsel (helping you get healthy again), God's intervention, and time.

Even your former husband will expect you to get over it after some time has passed. Remember when I told you that Fred, Wilma, and I happened to be on the same flight to attend a family event? When my brother picked me up at the airport, Fred said, "You didn't have to make Tom come all the way here to get you. Wilma and I are renting a car and would have been happy to drop you off." *Helllooo! Are you serious?* Did he really think I wanted to be in the back-seat of the car like Jessica Tandy in *Driving Miss Daisy* and be chauffeured by them for forty-five minutes while we made small talk? I think not! This is what I call "The Clue-less Syndrome."

There will be new hurts you face after the divorce is finalized. They're the ripple effects. Take the water-filter episode I had. After my divorce, I moved into my new home, and the water filter in my refrigerator needed replacing. Supposedly, it just screwed out of the bottom, and you screwed a new one back in to replace it. I tried and tried to unscrew the dang thing. I took a wrench to it to get it loose, and it wouldn't budge. I tried this for days and gave up. Well, a week or so later, a workman came over to fix the fireplace, and I mustered up the courage to ask him to unscrew the water filter. He came right over and unscrewed it immediately with no trouble at all. I stood there with tears streaming down my face because I felt so helpless and so weak. The guy must've thought I was a nut case.

Truthfully, some of my grief may never completely end because we have children together, and we must find a way to cope. With each holiday or special event, all the old feelings are dredged up again. There are days I feel great, and it seems like I've taken a few steps forward. Then something will happen that will make the pain resurface, and I take a couple of steps backward. That's when I go to the cross again and ask Jesus to give me His heart and help me get past this.

To be completely honest, I had new hurt because my children accepted my husband's new marriage. They were so angry when it first happened, but now that it's over and done with and he's remarried, they've accepted the situation for what it is. I wanted them to "dis" the two of them because doing that would show their disapproval. But the truth is I'm glad my children have a decent relationship with their father. In fact, he has been a better dad and much more attentive to the girls since the divorce because he knows how horrible they feel, and he's trying to make it right.

I have been guilty of telling the girls how badly I feel and of saying some nasty things. I thought they could handle it because they're adults now, and because this divorce deal was his decision. Take my advice: Do *not* do this! You will drive your kids away from you. You must hold your tongue and take the gripes and hurts to a friend, your pastor, or your counselor. Your adult kids don't want to hear your complaints. After all, he is their dad.

So, if you're divorced and there's another woman in the picture and you have joint custody or even if your children are grown, as mine are, and you have to share your kids for holidays or be in the same room with the new family unit for special family events, you will have to find a way to come to terms with this situation for your sake and for the kids. This does not mean you have to be pals with your former husband and his significant other. You just have to learn to be gracious. What a difficult task it is. But it can be done with God's grace.

On an entirely practical note, this is a good time to make a will if you don't have one, or change the one you have. Seven out of ten adults are walking around without a will, and it's just not responsible. I knew a man who was on his third marriage. He had four children from previous marriages. His third wife was twenty-five years younger than he was. They were married for three years when he died unexpectedly. He didn't make the necessary changes to his will, and wife No. 3 got everything he had. She gave zilch to his four children. So, always be prepared. Make sure all your insurance is in order. Don't forget disability insurance. Now that you're on your own, you'll need that. A good financial planner is a must. Find a good recommendation from someone you know. This person can help you set up financial goals for your future and your retirement.

On the self-esteem and personal-worth front, the road to recovery can be slow. You've probably lost a little weight. Most of us can write a book called *The Divorce Diet*, but what a lousy way to slim down! You can't eat because you're constantly nauseated. You're wondering if men still find you attractive. You hope you can still turn their heads your way. This is where we

CONNIE'S LIFE LESSONS
The After-Divorce Stage

Many of us suffer from PTSD (Post Traumatic Stress Disorder) from our divorces and the life changes that go with them. That's why a good run of counseling is very much in order. You may say, "I can't afford to do it." Honestly, you can't afford not to. Check around. There are some therapists who will work with you. You may have to go to a couple of different ones before you find someone you click with. And please don't be embarrassed for being in counseling. Instead, realize that almost the entire population needs some counseling from time to time—even counselors themselves. So be encouraged that you're working toward getting healthy.

really have to be careful. Basically, we're starving for affection and approval from men. We want to be desired and loved again. We are so vulnerable now, and that is dangerous. Don't do what I did. I got tangled up (not literally!) with the yoga instructor with the long blond Fabio hair.

We gals are so emotionally based that we can make horrible decisions if we only trust our emotions. Our brains—and our spirits—have to be engaged if we are to make wise decisions about future relationships.

Learning to trust again will be difficult for all of us. We don't want to hurt like this anymore so it's a good thing to be cautious. You will know when and whom you can trust again at the right time. Your life is not over . . . it's just different. Always have a dream. A vision. A goal. It doesn't matter how small or large it is. Just have one. Without a dream, you die inside.

So to sum it up, what's life like after divorce? Well, it just might become the best thing that ever happened to you.

Rosalind

"Life After Divorce. Yeah, Right!"

Reflecting back, I remember hearing the words, "There is life after divorce." This was the message that was given to me from a salesperson in the jewelry store when I told her I was there to return the expensive watch I purchased for my husband for Valentine's Day. I explained to her that I no longer needed the watch because the man I bought it for had announced that he was leaving me. After I gave her the watch and the receipt, I was so upset that I began to sob. The tears were streaming down my face. Putting the watch aside, she grabbed my hand and passed me a tissue. With compassion, she began to disclose her life regarding her own divorce.

Now this is the part I couldn't comprehend. Toward the end of the conversation, she said these words to me: "There is life after divorce."

I looked at her and said, "I don't think so because my heart is aching and my world is falling apart. It's impossible for me to see that right now."

Well, that conversation took place six years ago, and now I can say she was absolutely right. There is life after divorce. Abundant life, even. I have great days, good days, not so good days, and even bad days, but I'm still here. I'm a survivor, and you will be a survivor, too.

As for single parenting . . . wow, I never dreamed I would be a single parent. It's a tough role when you're doing it alone. However, I do what I have to do to make sure my son's needs are met and his environment is safe and secure. I was raised in a two-parent home, so I struggled with being a single parent because both of my parents were there for me, and that's what I wanted for my son. Nevertheless, we are blessed despite the choices that were made. Yes, I'm a single parent, and the job can be hard at times, but I'm so thankful just to be a parent.

ROSALIND'S LIFE LESSONS
The After-Divorce Stage

Since divorce, my relationship with God has become special to me. I have the desire to spend time with Him and a genuine thirst for His Word. I have gone from being "religious" to having a personal relationship with Him. The rejection, brokenness, and pain drew me closer to the Lord. So now my primary focus is to walk in the purpose and plan God has for me. This is a perfect time for you, too, to foster a relationship with God or restore your relationship with Him. He is waiting with open arms to comfort you and heal you from your pain, but you have to allow Him to. My question is, are you willing to allow Him to heal you?

Raising a son with his father living far away is difficult because my son doesn't have the opportunity to really bond with his father like he wants to. Yes, his father provides for him financially, and he is in his life. However, my son wishes his father was closer so they could spend quality time together. Thankfully, since his father is so far away, the special men in my life—my father, my brothers, and a couple of male friends—all play an important role in his life.

As for me and my needs, *dating* wasn't even in my vocabulary after my divorce. I didn't want a man near me, especially one who was interested in a serious relationship. Since I was still hurting and vulnerable, I didn't want to attract men who were in the same state I was because it's just unsafe. Misery loves company. I've learned to prayerfully wait on God to send my "Boaz" or "Isaac" or whatever his name will be! I am a "Lady in Waiting," trying to be content to be near the King.

I've made mistakes and I still make mistakes, but I don't allow myself to stay in condemnation for the ones I've made. Every day, my goal is to become a whole and complete woman. I want to be healed from within. I thank God for His amazing grace, something I don't deserve. But He gives it to me every day, and He has forgiven me and will continue to forgive me for all the mistakes I've made. He is a God of second chances. If you need more chances, He will extend them to you, too. My point is He will not give up on you. He will never leave you nor forsake you. He never breaks His promises. (Can I get a witness?)

Here is one of my favorite Scriptures: "All things (the good, the bad, and the ugly) work together for the good of those who love the Lord and are called according to His purpose" (see Rom. 8:28). Rest on this promise and know there is life after divorce.

Carla

"Isn't This Ironic?"

I'm looking in the mirror and thinking to myself, *How in the world am I going to pull this off—a job interview after years of diaper duty and* Teletubbies? On the outside I looked pretty darn good, if I do say so myself. By this time, I was down more than sixty pounds and wearing a svelte size ten. For

you "Skinny Minnies" this isn't a big deal, but for us southern gals raised on fried chicken and biscuits, this is monumental. I don't think I even wore a size ten when I was ten!
I had on my new powder-blue suit, my power hairdo, and I
was ready to take on the world, right? Wrong! On the inside, I was a quivering little child who just wanted to go
back to bed and pretend that "this" was happening to someone else.

Life after divorce is so ironic. You have to make some of
the most important decisions in your life—legal, financial,
personal, career—when emotionally you really aren't capable of deciding "paper or plastic" at the grocery store. Here
I was going for a job interview where you have to "sell
yourself" and be confident when I felt like the biggest loser
in the world. Don't get me wrong, I was no stranger to hard
work, and I knew I had a good résumé and skills, but I was
a nervous wreck and pretty much broke out in hives at my
prospects. I had held a job since my paper route at age four-
teen, but this time it was different. The "plan" had always
been for me to be the breadwinner while my husband got
his flight hours, and then I would stay at home with the babies until they went to school. I was even going to transition from a marketing career to a teaching career at that
time. *Daycare* was practically a four-letter word in our
house. Now I had to get a job, find suitable daycare, and get
ready to move out of the house within six weeks.

If you are going back to work, I highly recommend a job
that doesn't take a lot of brain power and a boss who un-

derstands you might be missing some time due to court appearances, real estate matters, insurance, children adjusting to daycare issues, afternoon crying sessions, and chocolate binges. Oh, and don't forget about tax time. I had never been audited in my life, but there must be someone at the IRS who flags the "divorcee" returns and decides that the woman just hasn't been through enough, so let's question her return. It was priceless, absolutely priceless. (For the record, I did "win" and received my money with interest. I praise God for my CPA and his staff. It was money well-spent.)

Speaking of spending money—don't. Really, this is no time for shopping therapy (or only the minimum level of shopping therapy). I found myself using credit cards like there was no tomorrow. Miss "Debt-Free Living" and Dave Ramsey-wannabe was "Discovering" and "Mastering" all kinds of pretty things. Visa was everywhere I wanted to be. My rationale was that when I moved out, I couldn't bear to take things that held so many memories. I'm telling you now, take it. Paint it if you have to, decoupage it, sell it, whatever. Those things are expensive and difficult to replace.

I also spent out of guilt, trying to replace the "things" my babies had at their "old house" and keep up with Disneyland Dad. Seriously, women use that term to describe an ex-husband who spoils the kids out of guilt for the divorce, but my husband actually took them to Disney World.

Life after divorce is a time of such vulnerability. From

the "older" gentleman who just wants to "be there for you" and sends you cuddly teddy bears and cards about how God will take care of you to the young whippersnapper who propositions you in the Sam's Club parking lot, you may get a lot of unwanted attention that is uncomfortable to deal with. I ended up buying a wedding band just to wear and fend off prospective suitors. I'm not saying it wasn't a little bit nice having the attention, especially since I had been with the same man for all of my adult life; but please know that I agree with my fellow authors: when you are newly divorced, this is not a time to start any type of romantic relationship. I made mistakes in this area as I tried to recapture the security and love I had lost. I was naïve and gullible, and I still regret some pretty stupid decisions I made during this time. Thankfully, we have a God of grace and mercy and a Savior whose blood washes away all of the bad stuff. And once your slate is clean, and you have a sense of the new "you" and what you want out of life, then you will be more adept at dating.

One of my favorite memories of "life after divorce" was when my children and I were sitting in our little apartment eating dinner and trying to ignore some noisy teenagers outside our window. I told my precious toddlers that one day God would bring a wonderful man into Mommy's life who would love her and be a wonderful stepdaddy and go to church with us. My four-year-old son pondered this for a while and then said, "What about the Domino's Pizza guy?" I began to laugh hysterically as I thought about it from his point of view. All you had to do was call, he came running, and he brought steaming hot pepperoni pizza. Of course he was the perfect guy for Mommy!

That laugh was very therapeutic. Find the bright side of things, and try to laugh a lot. It's certainly better than all that crying!

After divorce, as in all of life, there are highs and lows. One minute you're facing the fact that you really should be tested for sexually transmitted diseases if your husband had other partners. The next minute you're at the park blowing bubbles and laughing with your kids because now you know how very precious every moment with them really is. The bad stuff you've been through really has a way of illuminating the good. So focus on the good stuff as much as you can, and give the bad stuff to God.

CARLA'S LIFE LESSONS
The After-Divorce Stage

Even though we feel like losers sometimes because we are now in the category of "divorced woman," we are the norm since the divorce rate has exceeded the 50 percent mark. (Doesn't that make you feel better? Not!) Consider this: You get to learn lots of new things and even do a lot of homework, as you learn to appreciate the world of finances, taxes, insurance, wills, and remote control programming. You may have been able to turn these things over to your husband before. Now it's time to expand your horizons and allow yourself to feel good that you are doing something to take care of yourself.

Life after divorce is pretty much a balancing act some days. Remind yourself how delicate the balance is by walking across a room a couple of times on a tightrope with a potato on your shoe, a book on top of your head, and a glass of water in the palm of each hand. Do this while at least one of your kids is tugging at your sleeve (smile).

Seriously, when you are learning to balance all of your new roles, beg God for grace and give yourself some. Remember that you are on a steep learning curve, so don't condemn yourself when all the balls you are juggling come tumbling down. When it happens, just pick them up, dust them off, and start tossing them into the air again.

Final Thoughts

We have found that life after divorce should be all about getting healthy again, managing your new life, finding a way to accept it, and beginning to enjoy it. Look at the good things in your new life, even little things like keeping the light on by the bed as long as you want to because you're engrossed in that great book you can't put down. And remember what God has promised you in His Word. He says, "So I will restore to you the years that the swarming locust has eaten." (Joel 2:25 NKJV). Your future may someday involve another man, or it may not. But if you stay on the path God has laid down for your life, you will

In the area of finding balance, one thing that can help tremendously is organization. If your house, like your life, has become a mess, borrow some really good friends for a day or hire a professional organizer and get your house in order. Clean out the cabinets and closets. Organize your clothes and the kids' clothes by colors or outfits, so that on the rough days, you can just grab and go without really having to think about it.

A thorough housecleaning can make you feel like you have accomplished something worthwhile and give you an extra boost on days when you feel overwhelmed.

have life and have it more abundantly than ever. Whatever the outcome, it will be God's best for you. Believe that, and trust in His promises for your life.

Yes, life after divorce can be sometimes good, bad, and even ugly, but most of the time that will depend on you and the choices you make as you navigate this new life. We speak from experience. You can do this. Remember your mantra:

I will live.

I will laugh.

And, yes, I will love again!

Five Action Steps for a
Fantastic Future After Divorce

1. We know you've heard this before, but make sure that you have a good network of people to help you from time to time. This will help alleviate some of the pressures of life, since everyone needs a break and someone to care.
2. If you've never been an organized person, learn now to manage your life more efficiently. It may be tough at first, as your powers of concentration are probably shot. Don't be shocked if you find the butter in your coat closet or the mail in your refrigerator. Things can get pretty chaotic.
3. Learn to laugh at yourself. It's great medicine. Embrace humor. Hang out with people who will encourage you. Don't surround yourself with complainers and negative people. Do plan time with friends for an activity you enjoy—something that gets you out of your usual routine. Ballroom dancing, anyone?
4. Appreciate God's creation. Take a walk and look at the flowers, trees, and blue sky. Check out the beach or the mountains, and notice the birds and the squirrels. God cared enough to create all this beauty and take care of it. How much more will He take care of you, someone created "in His image"?
5. Relax. Many times, with all that tightrope walking and plate spinning we do, that's easier said than done. Try

anyway. Rotate your shoulders and move your head from side to side to stretch those taut neck muscles. Take some deep breaths (not enough to hyperventilate) several times a day. Drink lots of water (It alleviates headaches.), take your vitamins, and rest whenever you can. Indulge in a nap on Sunday afternoon while the kids watch a video. Give yourself permission to rest.

Survival Checklist

Dos and Don'ts for Post-Divorce Success

* *Do* stay in counseling. Try at least a six-month run with someone you "click" with.

* *Do* have your counselor/therapist work with you on setting boundaries—those protective walls that keep you from being hurt again. Enough is enough!

* *Do* read that Bible (even sleep with it open and pressed against your chest!). The words will penetrate into your heart and soul giving you comfort, peace and hope.

* *Do* make a "Build-a-Bear" to sleep with. Laugh if you have to, but hanging on to that teddy bear at night does help.

* *Do* stay in God's Word and pray.

* *Do* go to a spa and get a facial or a pedicure.

* *Do* take it one day at a time.

* *Don't* sleep with your ex, or anyone else for that matter. It will only bring more hurt and pain. Remember, there

are men looking for vulnerable women to prey on, and there are men who are just as messed up and hurting as you. Right now your face has "needy" written all over it.

✳ *Don't* make a habit of letting your kids sleep in your room/bed.

✳ *Don't* keep rehashing the past, trying to figure out how you could have done it differently. It's time to move forward.

✳ *Don't* put all the blame on him. Likewise, don't take all the blame. It takes two to marry *and* divorce.

✳ *Don't* find ways to make his life miserable. " 'Vengeance is Mine, I will repay,' says the Lord" (Hebrews 10:30 NKJV).

✳ *Don't* put your kids in the roles of confidante or counselor.

✳ *Don't* expect your older or adult children to feel about their dad the way you do. Remember, he didn't divorce them. He divorced you.

✳ *Don't* "bad mouth" your ex to the children. It can work against you and drive them away from you instead of toward you.

✳ *Don't* make an extravagant purchase right now, when you aren't thinking clearly yet. No new car, new house . . . not even new breasts (smile)!

✳ And the biggest "Do" of all: Repeat the following: *I will live, I will laugh, and, yes, I will love again!*

Chapter 8

A New Day!–Live, Laugh, Love Again

This is the day the LORD has made;
We will rejoice and be glad in it.

—*Psalm 118:24 NKJV*

We want to leave you with stories of our lives now and our advice for the future. We would like to say everything is simply awesome, that our lives and our skin have never looked better, that we eat right, are the perfect size, and have wonderful men who wait on us hand and foot. But we live in reality, and the real world is never the fairy tale. You know what we learned? We'd actually rather have our bumps and bruises anyway. Sure, the pain and struggle can be a major drag, but without the tragedy in our lives, we would never know what it feels like to triumph!

Does our current heartache make us exempt from future heartache? All together now: No! But can we rest assured that God will work everything for good when we trust Him? Yes! While it is hard to see beyond today when you are in the throes of a divorce, hang onto the saying "This too shall pass." It really is so true. Time heals the broken-hearted, and the memories will fade as you move forward in your new life. New memories will replace the old, maybe not altogether, but for the most part.

For some it is tougher than others, but healing does come. You are a lot more resilient than you think. One last time, we want you to know you are not alone. Women all over the world have gone through the same pain you are experiencing or have experienced, and they have pulled through. You can do it. We are your cheerleaders, and we are here to encourage, educate, and walk beside you (in spirit, if not in the flesh) while you rebuild your life.

Just the comfort in knowing someone understands you, has walked in your shoes, and has had to face the same pain and darkness can be a wonderful revelation. It helps you to know you are not crazy, you are not a loser, and you are not going to stay in your situation because God is going to help you move forward. He will guide you and give you wisdom to take the next step in your life. We certainly hope more than anything that this book has been a source of healing for you. This is what it means to "Live, Laugh, and Love Again." It means healing, restoration, and forgiveness.

It is not easy to learn to trust again, to learn to sing

again, to learn to have joy again, but you will. Keep in mind that this life is so short. In only a moment, we will be in heaven with our Lord; so don't waste any time! Put the past behind you, and make it your goal to get healthy. Continually ask yourself, "How can I get better?" and "What can I learn from this journey I have had to take?"

We are praying for you and asking God to help you come back from the pit of hell to the land of the living. A taste of the dark side is plenty, thank you. You don't want to live there. God is with you, holding you tightly in the palms of His hands. Do not be afraid, dear sisters, for He will be your guide. Look to Him for answers and you will find them.

Michelle

"The Road Too Well-Traveled"

During my pain, during the darkest moments of my divorce, I truly never thought I would live, laugh, and love again. I couldn't even imagine my life beyond the tragic and painful circumstances I was in. Never before had I felt so hopeless. My optimistic nature was dampened. In fact, there was not even one bit of optimism left in me when my husband of thirteen years said to me, "I want a divorce." I couldn't see the rainbow on the other side of the mountain. I couldn't even see the front door, because I'd retreated so far under my bed.

Even when I hid, even in all the hopelessness, there was

this little voice in me, deep inside, saying, "You will survive. You will survive." No, it wasn't Gloria Gaynor on "repeat" in the CD player (smile). It was God; He was telling me I would make it. He was there when I had no one, and He was the only one who saw into me and knew my pain.

He will find you if you are willing to be found. In the beginning stages of my divorce, I was such a wreck that I didn't want to see anyone for about six months. I really went nowhere—not to church, not to dinner, not anywhere but work. I couldn't even go shopping! That's how bad it was, girls. I didn't call anyone, and no one called me. I was hiding out. I felt like a big fat zero, a big fat failure; and I didn't want to face the world, family, God, or anyone else.

I remember one night it was late and I had ordered pizza for the kids. We had been waiting quite some time when finally there was a knock on the door. Of course, we all thought it was the pizza guy. Excitedly, all five of us went to the door to answer, very anxious to smell the wonderful scent of a good steaming pie delivered right to our front step.

I opened the door and there stood this delightful woman. Before I could even get a word out, she immediately went in to her spiel, telling me all about the many different magazines she had for sale. She was one of those door-to-door magazine salespeople who raise money for schools. All I could think of while she was chatting away was, *How am I going to get her off my porch so I can shut the door and get back to my haven inside?*

I patiently waited as she rambled on about the magazines, and how if she got just one more sale she would be on a trip to Jamaica or something like that. At that point, I didn't care about her life or her trip to Jamaica. I was having a full-blown pity party. Couldn't she see that? Besides, I was the one who deserved the darn trip to Jamaica.

I blurted out, "Listen, I just went through a divorce and can barely afford to keep things afloat right now. I'm sorry, but I just can't help you." As I began to close the door, she asked me to wait just a moment. "Forget about the magazines," she said. "Can I pray for you?" Before I could even reply, she quickly grabbed me and wrapped her strong arms around me. My kids, who had been huddled around watching intensely, immediately gathered together and put their little hands on my shoulders as she began to pray.

I have always imagined going to one of those awesome African-American churches in the South, with the music blarin' and the choir belting out praise songs. Well, I can tell you, God brought that church to me in the encouragement of this beautiful lady. She shouted over me and prayed a prayer like she was standing right before Jesus Himself. By the time she was done there were tears streaming down my face, and I was hugging her neck like she was my best friend from back home or something. Whew, what a prayer that was!

When she was done praying, she simply told me to keep her in my prayers, said she would do the same for me, and walked off into the darkness. I can't wait to see her in heaven one day. That woman changed my life as God used her to let me know that even if He had to come to my door, He would find me.

He did find me, and He has restored my life. It's not a perfect life, but a restored one. I have remarried, but my restoration has nothing to do with a new man in my life. Yes, I am so pleased to have found someone I can love and who loves me, but restoration after divorce is beyond re-marriage. It is the healing of the torn flesh, the ability to have joy and happiness that enables us to truly live again. It is only the work of the Lord in our hearts, the deep work of the Holy Spirit in our lives, that can truly restore all that has been lost. What has been broken must be rebuilt. This can only be done if we allow God to come into the deep places in our soul and fill them with His love for us. It is His gift to us, His restoration and healing. We must receive it if we want to have it.

A dear friend, who is so affirming, sent me an e-mail telling me how truly beautiful I am, speaking into my life, and letting me know what a treasure I am. This affirmation, this love, made me think of the love of the Father and how truly He and He alone can fill my deepest longings. I feel great in my forties to be able to say, "I am truly loved." The deepest longing in my heart is being met, not by a man, my dad, my friends, or even my kids, but by a precious God who loves me beyond what I could ever imagine. He wants the best for me; He wants the best for us. No one can take that away. He will never abandon us, and it is in giving ourselves to Him and His wonderful Word that we will truly find the restoration we are looking for, the healing we are looking for, and the love we are looking for. After coming through my divorce, I realize there is no one who can truly know you, understand you, and love you the way God does.

In closing, I want to say that you never really get over a divorce, but you do get beyond it. Life moves on, and you can let that train drag you behind it, or you can board it and go places you hadn't expected. Either way, you're gonna be moving. I chose to move on and to open my heart again.

I would be lying to you if I said I'm totally fine. There is still a hole in my heart, but it gets smaller as time goes on. There are still moments when I hear a certain song, see a movie, visit a city, that remind me of the life I had with my former husband, and for a moment sadness comes over me. But the moment always passes quickly. I am happy again, not because I'm married or because life is going perfect, but because "I know that I know that I know" that I can get through anything with God's help.

I still see my former husband every month when he picks up the kids, but I no longer well up in tears after he leaves. I no longer wonder how things would have been "if only." I no longer dwell on how I wish things could have been. Instead, I think about how glad I am that we have these four beautiful children, about how wonderful they are, and how my former husband and I have moved into the realm of "cordial" acquaintances. It's kind of bizarre after fifteen years of sharing a life and many years of sharing a bed. But we can hold a polite conversation and go on our way. We are even moving from cordial to friendly, and he works with me to do what is best for our children.

I know divorce was never what God intended, but it is what it is. Now God requires us to put others first, to love unconditionally, to set aside our own selfish desires and pride for the sake of our children.

That's what He wants you to do, to hop up on the train of life and grab a seat near the window while He takes you on a glorious ride. Here is a letter from the Lord to you. Take these words, and hide them in your heart. Say them over and over in your mind, and know His love for you is so great. You are His precious child, a princess of the King of Kings:

> My dear little one,
> You, my love, are a delight in my eyes. I have watched you all your life, and I have seen your pain, your difficulties. I have stood by and loved you with an everlasting love. All of the things no one sees, I see. I see how you hurt at night when no one is around. I see the tears that fall to the ground and seem to never end. I see each deep wound in your heart, and I see the places where you have been so hurt that anger has taken root.
>
> My precious one, know that I am God. Know that I and I alone can bring healing to your life. Know how much I want you to have all the things I desire to give. Know I can help you down the journey of forgiveness.
>
> I know it seems unfair, I know all you are disap-

pointed in, and I am here for you, walking beside you, guiding you in your footsteps. I will be your husband this day. I will be your covering. Toss your shame away; toss away your pain. This is a new day, and on this day, I will restore all that has been lost. You, my darling, are loved. You are loved so deeply. I am wrapping my arms around you. Come and rest in my lap and know I am here to hold you. When no one can hear you, I hear. I hear the screams of pain crying out in your soul, and I am here to soothe you.

My love, look to me, seek me and you will find me.

You are so beautiful, so lovely, so unconditionally loved by Me.

Love,
Your Father, Your Messiah, and Your God

Don't you forget these words! When you walk by a mirror and you stop and look at yourself, know He loves you. You are "beautifully and wonderfully made" (see Ps. 139:14). Your loss is great. My loss was great. But it is not the end of your life as it was not the end of mine. It is simply a new beginning to another chapter. Be encouraged, have hope, and be strong, for you, my friends, will live again, laugh again, and love again.

Connie

"A Long Way in a Short Time"

When you go through pain, it seems like it lasts for eternity. You think, *Will it ever end?* I remember when my firstborn had colic. There was nothing I could do to console her. She screamed day and night. I felt so inadequate as a new mother. I asked God why He had allowed me to be a mom if I couldn't even make my baby stop crying. I couldn't wait for that colic to end. It lasted for nine months. It felt like forever. Today, she is a beautiful woman, and the time seems to have gone by in the blink of an eye.

Like I asked God about the colic, twenty-three years later I asked Him why He allowed me to become a wife if I couldn't make my marriage work. I may never fully understand in this life, but I know that I have learned good things, and drawn closer to my God because of it. Life has been a myriad of huge adjustments, but I am making them with His grace, with His love. He provided a network of friends that supported me and held my hand and loved me during this horrible time in my life. He gave me His Word and His promises that have stood the test of time and have proven true in my life. I thank God for His provision and grace. He is my constant companion, friend, lover, counselor, attorney, accountant, husband, redeemer, savior and my Lord.

What an education it is to be a divorced woman! There's no college degree for this one. I'm a lot smarter about financial issues. I actually know how to pay bills (Don't laugh!), keep my own business records, and make sound business decisions. I now have good working relationships with my financial planner, banker, accountant, attorney, and insurance agents. I'm making it on my own. I've made new friends. I'm doing some traveling and going places I've never gone before. God has opened up ministry and career opportunities for me as well.

Everything I thought had died within me for good was not actually dead, but dormant, and has come back to life again. I've taken a few classes. I do what I want, when I want, wherever I want, with whomever I want. Actually, I'm doing much better than I thought. I have eased into my new life very nicely. The journey has been bumpy at times, to say the least, but there have been some very nice patches along the way.

And . . . I'm slowly trying out a new relationship. I'm proceeding with caution.

In all honesty, my life didn't turn out the way I'd hoped it would. I'd hoped I'd grow old with Fred—holding hands in the rocking swing on the front porch admiring my garden and watching the grandbabies frolicking on our beautifully manicured lawn. I'd hoped our children would live close to home so Fred and I could baby-sit our grandbabies together. I'd hoped we'd all be together often and my girls and their husbands and children would all come over for a big Italian family dinner every Sunday after church. I'd hoped that when my daughters got married that I'd be sitting with Fred instead of another woman being at his side.

No, it didn't turn out the way I'd expected. But you know what? It's still all good. I'm going to be all right. I've sur-

vived—no, triumphed—over one of the most difficult bat-
tles of my life. I was thrown a curve ball, and by golly, I hit
it out of the park! Yes, I'm on that winning path and I'm running for home. This time I'm going to make it. I will win.

We all win when we're on the right team. Frankly, you
can't lose when you're on the path God intended for you. No,
I'm sure that for most of us it wasn't His ultimate will that
we divorce, but it happened. Here's where we can prove Romans 8:28 to be true for us: "For we know that *all* things
work together for good to those who love God, to those who
are the called according to His purpose" (NKJV, italics mine).

I also know now that it's all based on the choices I make.
I can either choose to serve God or not. I can choose pain,
suffering, sorrow, anger, and sadness; or I can choose peace,
faith, joy, forgiveness, and love. So every day, before I get
out of my bed, I make a conscious effort to choose the
good things. I choose to win.

Now the ball's in your court, and we're all cheering
for you!

Rosalind

"A New Day"

Wow, I am actually living, laughing, and open to loving
again! The heartache I once felt is no longer there. Each area
of my life (emotionally, mentally, physically, and spiritually)
is somewhat balanced now. I am not as overwhelmed as I

was in the beginning of my journey of healing. Overall, I can say I have stability in my life. Sister, you, too, will have this in your life. Just don't give up. I say this from experience: Keep persevering. Yes, it will be overwhelming in the beginning, middle, and maybe at the end; but know it will come to pass. And along the way, God will reveal His hand at work in your life in ways you have never seen before.

When I was going through my divorce, I participated in a divorce support group at my church. Girls, that was a place of refuge every Wednesday night. I knew the place was safe, and I received support from my peers. Although we all had different stories, we related well to one another because of what we were experiencing. When the facilitator decided that she was going into counseling full time, she asked *me* if I would be open to leading the next group of Divorce Care enrollees. I told her that I definitely would be in prayer about facilitating a group of people because I had never led a class before in my life! Let me tell you, fear crept in because I felt I was not capable of fulfilling that position. My self-confidence was shot during that time. In my prayer time I confessed to the Lord that I was afraid, but I was going to step out in faith and trust Him. He gave me this faith assignment because He knew I could do it, even though I had my doubts.

Sisters, please know that these opportunities will come your way, too, so that you can be a testimony to His glory. Years later, I am still one of the facilitators for the divorce recovery support group at my church. And I love doing what I do! There is no doubt in my mind that God placed me in this ministry. In each class I see myself as witness to what God can bring you through if you allow Him to.

He also blessed me with a wonderful friend in ministry. After I confirmed that I would be open to taking the group over, I asked if I could have someone assist me, since I had never led a group before. My facilitator had someone in mind, but I didn't know her. When we met, we clicked, and not only did I get someone to assist me with the support group, but I also gained a wonderful, godly friend who is a blessing to me. We have a beautiful friendship, which is something you need when you are going through a divorce.

As for the future, it has always been a desire of mine to get my master's degree in Social or Behavioral Sciences. Instead of pursing my dream, I put it on hold when I got married. Sisters, I know some of you can relate to that. After getting confirmation after confirmation, God opened the doors. Even as a single mom with fears that school would take me away from my son too much or put us in the poorhouse, God made a way. He came through every time.

There continue to be challenging times that have required me to be still and trust Him. There was one particular time I needed someone to watch my son when my support system was not available. I took that issue to God because I began to panic. Let me tell you, my prayer was answered that same night.

I am thankful for my relationship with God, who has made provision for me. I am also thankful for my son, who supports me. When it is all said and done, I think about

Philippians 3:12-14: "I am not saying that I have this all to-gether, that I have it made. But I am well on my way, reaching out for Christ, who has so wondrously reached out to me. Friends, do not get me wrong: by no means do I count myself an expert in all of this, but I've got my eye on the goal, where God is beckoning us onward—to Jesus. I'm off and running, and I'm not turning back" (MESSAGE).

I am able to live, laugh, and love again. You will be able to soon.

Carla

"I'm Going to Make It"

I agree with Nicole Johnson in her book *Keeping a Princess Heart in a Not-So-Fairy-Tale World*—Walt Disney really messed us up. Like Cinderella and Sleeping Beauty, we still love and long for a happy ending. On the outside we may be strong women, but on the inside some of us are just little girls who want our Prince Charming to come and rescue us from all of life's drudgery. We're convinced that if we just have the right guy, then all will be well. After my divorce and several unsuccessful dating relationships, I found myself saying that if I just met the "right one" then I would have that "perfect" life. Right? Wrong!

It has taken two failed marriages for me to realize no person can be my prince. There is no man on this earth who can truly fill this hole inside my heart. People will fail you—this, sisters, we know all too well. If there is anything I have learned in life, it is God and only God who will never fail us, never let us down, and well, teach us to laugh at ourselves in the process of it all.

Through all the pain I have endured over these past few years, the one thing I have not lost is my faith! I do praise God that I have continued to stay in church and surround myself with some really great women who have been there for me through my heartache. I am not going to tell you that I have no desire to remarry, or to meet the man of my dreams. I have to be honest with you. And, most important, be real! I still pray I will meet the man of my dreams. But I am not looking for him. I am content in focusing on my relationship with God and my children. They are my purpose, and I am investing in them with everything I am.

If God does bring me a man, the only thing I request is a burning bush as a signal to know it is okay for me to go out with him. That's not too much to ask, is it (smile)? Seriously, my girlfriends, have an application and a lie detector test waiting.

In the meantime I feel great knowing I can make it on my own, knowing the road ahead is something to be excited about, like an adventure waiting to be unveiled. For the first time in my life, I get to set goals for myself. I guess all of us, when we are in a marriage that is suffering, tend to want to focus on the other person and the help they need. Now that there is no other person, focus on the help you need. Focus on getting yourself in order and healthy. Set goals for yourself that you feel are attainable and work toward those.

Michelle told me about a friend who is a successful counselor. She herself is divorced, and, honey, if there is anyone who should be bitter and angry it would be her. Her story is one of major heartache. As a result of the major difficulty she had in forgiveness, this amazing counselor made it her life journey to help women deal with acceptance. In the latter part of her life she has managed to pick up the pieces of her divorce, get her degree and then her doctorate, and begin helping women who have endured this tragic pain. She has counseled so many women from all different backgrounds, with so many different stories, and the one thing they all have in common is the root of unforgiveness. She says their stories may not start out revealing the unforgiveness, but by the time she is through with them, it is revealed. She claims this unforgiveness causes mental issues, physical illness and, of course, keeps women from moving on.

As hard as it is—and believe me, sister, I cannot tell you how hard it has been for me—I urge you to work through it until it is finished!

It would be completely wrong for me to close this book telling you I have it all together, that I have somehow picked up all the pieces from my divorce and I look so great you could tie a bow on me and give me away as a gift. No, again, our goal with this book was to be real, and I must be real with you. I have had broken relationships that have left me devastated, I have continued to deal with my ex-husband in court over our children, and the aftermath of di-

vorce left me financially devastated as well. But in all of
that, I will say, I have gone deeper in my relationship with
God, and like Job I am very confident my Lord will restore
to me (and to you) all that has been lost. Remember, our
Lord has plans to prosper us and not to harm us (see Jer.
29:11). So continue to keep the faith.

In closing, although my heart has been absolutely broken into pieces in different times in my life, I take comfort
in knowing God always knows the outcome and I take hope
in knowing He will work it for His good, even if we don't
understand it at the time. Along those lines, I love the Bible
devotion by Elisabeth Elliot that says:

> One morning I was reading the story of Jesus' feeding
> of the five thousand. The disciples could find only
> five loaves of bread and two fishes. "Let me have
> them," said Jesus. He asked for all. He took them, said
> the blessing, and broke them before he gave them
> out. I remembered what a chapel speaker, Ruth Stull
> of Peru, had said: "If my life is broken when given to
> Jesus, it is because pieces will feed a multitude, while
> a loaf will satisfy only a little lad."[5]

Right now you may be broken, you may be scattered in
pieces, but trust in the fact God will use it for His glory, and
that He and He alone will put together the pieces of your
life and feed the multitudes. Plus, this journey of yours will
someday be spiritual nourishment for a friend in her own
moment of need. So don't be afraid, when the healing

comes (and it will) to share with others the journey you have walked, so that they too may be healed.

Final Thoughts

We know that you will overcome. We know each one of you is going through tremendous pain and heartache, but we can attest to the fact that your heart will surely heal, you will live and not die, you will survive (as Gloria Gaynor so eloquently puts it), and you will keep living, laughing, and loving. It's all good! Trust us. We are the Fearsome Four, who jumped over buildings in a bound, climbed mountains and reached the top, fell down in the basement, and finally found the floor. We have almost drowned in the river of tears we cried, but we made it— we swam to shore! Hey, they don't call us "fearsome" for nothing. For it is in Him we live and move and have our being (see Acts 17:28), and it is in Him you will overcome and survive. Be blessed, girlfriends. Know that if we can do it, so can you! You will live, you will laugh, and you will love again.

Survival Checklist
Your New Life

Live

✳ Remember how important *balance* is in your life. Juggling work, children, household duties, socializing, and church events can be challenging and exhausting. Find friends who can help you in the day-to-day tasks. Other single moms are great because you can help one another. Believe us, there are plenty out there. Take time to be alone for self-reflection. It is easy to try to fill our calendars so we don't have to face what we have been through, but it is really only in the times of self-reflection that we can identify some of the issues we need to work on and get on with the process of healing.

* *Socialize* with good friends. You have been part of a couple, and now you are single. This will bring new opportunities for forming quality friendships that will last a lifetime. Find people you enjoy spending time with. After you are feeling healthy again, it may be a good time to start a support group of women who have gone through a divorce. It is so healing to be with others who can relate to your pain.

* Introduce *new things* into your life. Take a trip somewhere you've never gone before—even if it's just for a weekend. Go rock climbing, skiing, or do something creative and fun like painting.

* Be *healthy.* Eat right and exercise. This will help you feel good about yourself and keep your body well. Nutrition and exercise are so important when you are going through a divorce. It is too easy to fall into bad eating habits that cause weight gain or weight loss. All of us experienced this.

Laugh

✳ Find the *humor* in life. Laugh at yourself. It's great medicine. Watch funny movies, and stay away from anything depressing. Hang out with friends who love to have a good time, and just enjoy their company. Learn a new joke, and tell it to someone. Tickle your kids (This may be harder if they're adults!), and let them tickle you.

✳ According to *Health* magazine, laughing gives your body the same benefit as a workout and improves the blood flow in your arteries.[6] So give yourself a giggle fit and get fit giggling!

Love

✳ Be *sensible*. Don't rush into a serious relationship. Take time to get to know yourself. Then take time to get to know the man.

✳ *Learn* from the mistakes you made in your previous marriage. Be willing to explore the areas where you were wrong and ask God to refine your character.

✳ Don't forget *pre-marital counseling* if you're thinking about tying the knot again. Make sure that you have more than one or two sessions. Take plenty of time to cover all the bases—from the kids to the finances. You want to make sure you are not both bringing too many "ghosts of marriage" past into your new relationship.

✳ Make a *list* regarding all the things you expect from a man in your next relationship, and don't settle for anything less. Look for red flags. If there are any, you should re-think the relationship. Hopefully, you know you're not going to change him after you marry him.

✳ *Love yourself* before even thinking about loving someone else! Ask the Lord to reveal to you what a wonderful and special creature you are. Try to see yourself through His eyes, by reading the Bible verses that describe how He feels about you. (Did you know He is so excited about you that He sings? "He will exult over you by singing a happy song." Zeph. 3:17 NIV)

✳ *Read up* on the materials we list in the back of this book, and make sure you talk through any relationships with a counselor. Blended families and second marriages do not have high success rates for good reason. Educate yourself in every way before taking any steps toward becoming a stepfamily.

✳ Don't be *afraid* to love again when it is right. Fear is one of the greatest factors of failure in second and third marriages. You may get hurt again, but don't let not loving and trusting cripple you. If you do marry again, it is important the marriage is based on trust and unconditional love. This may take some time, but be patient. No one ever said love is easy, especially the next time around.

Authors' Note

Once you have gone through all the stages in this book and feel you are on your way to a healthy new you, write down your hopes and dreams on a piece of paper. List all of your desires and everything you wish for, including what you want for yourself, your children, and your relationships. Since this is a "New Day" for you, get down on your knees before the Lord and lay all these dreams down. Put all your desires at the foot of the cross by taking the piece of paper and laying it on the floor. Now pray this prayer with us:

Dear Jesus,

Remember me, oh Lord. Remember me, and restore all which has been lost. Help me to be patient, to wait on You. Lord, give me direction in making decisions, and help me to have wisdom when it comes to new relationships. Be the husband I do not have, be my covering when I am afraid, be a father to my children, and surround me with people who will help me in my times of need. Lord, continue to heal my heart. Continue to help me to forgive. When I am lonely, hold me in my pain. Lord, please help me every day to grow closer to You. I rejoice and thank You for helping me overcome, for helping me survive.

In Christ's name I pray, amen.

With Christ all these things are possible and more (see Mark 10:27). It is a new day, and all things are made new again. Be confident He will walk with you in your time of need, and know that He will carry you through when you feel you cannot go on. He will see you through, just as He has each one of us.

Please know that we love each and every one of you and pray God will help you work through the tremendous pain that comes as a result of divorce. We want you to have freedom from the aftermath of all that divorce brings, and we know you will! Know from our testimonies here that all you may be experiencing is normal. You are not crazy, you are not a loser, your life is not over, and we are all here to testify there is hope for tomorrow. May you be comforted by our words, and may you know after reading our stories that:

You *will* live.
You *will* laugh.
And, yes, you *will* love again.

We love you, sisters, and we identify with your pain! Let's move on together and begin this new journey of hope. Do we hear an "Amen, sister"?

In Christ,
Michelle, The Conz, Roz, and Carla Sue

A Checklist for Divorce

✳ Get a great attorney who not only knows about all the laws in your state and your rights, but also knows about money and what you will need and deserve. Your attorney is your new best friend. You need someone who can educate you regarding alimony, child support, and even health insurance issues.

✳ Forget any visions you may have of getting "your day in court" and embarrassing your spouse. Statistics show that only 5 percent of all divorces are fought out in court; the other 95 percent save money and time by coming to some agreement.[7] If there's any way you and your husband can agree on a settlement, you will save yourself much pain and money by not taking it to court.

✳ Stick up for your rights, and don't back down. Get what is fair and what you deserve—for your own sake and for the kids. We probably all know a friend who settled for less and struggled because of it. Don't underestimate your worth and contributions to the marriage. Even if you never worked out of the home, you contributed by being a dedicated wife and mother and by helping him achieve his goals in life. If he wants out, you are entitled to still live as well as you can. If he wants out, ask him to pay for all your legal fees.

✳ Think about health insurance. This is a big problem for a lot of women. Many were on their husbands' policies, and when they went to obtain their own were turned down, sometimes because of minor issues. In your divorce settlement, stipulate that he pay your health insurance for as long as possible, or see that he keeps you covered on his policy until you obtain something on your own.

✳ Secure disability income. Now that you're on your own and count on only your income, you need to have something in place should you not be able to work for a time. The bills will still need to be paid and the money won't be coming in, so figure the cost of all that into your alimony settlement.

✳ Decide who gets the house. Often it's us women who want the house, since we're the ones who invested so much time and energy into it. But we often can't afford to keep the house, or we don't want to live there alone, so we opt to sell. If you choose to let hubby keep the house or need to sell, make sure you get your share of the equity. You will also have tangible assets to split within the home.

* Consider college and other future events. Make sure that the children's college education is addressed in your settlement. If your children are girls, you may even need to suggest that you put it in writing how the weddings will be paid for.

* Form relationships with your banker, insurance agents, accountants, attorney, etc. Add a good financial planner to the mix to help you make the most out of your money.

* Make sure you know everything there is to know about all the financial aspects of your marriage—your credit cards, whose name is on the accounts, your taxes, insurance companies, outstanding debt, all your monthly bills, 401Ks, any other retirement accounts, savings and checking accounts, mutual funds, or any other investments you may have. If you are not sure, you may have to do a financial background check on your spouse. It's important for you to know everything. If you are not privy to this information, you could be liable for something years down the road that you had no knowledge of. Start doing your own investigative work, and keep accurate records of everything.

Appendix B

Tools for the Journey

One of the best things you can do during your alone time, especially the nights you can't sleep, is to delve into God's Word and other great resources so you can learn more about yourself and God's purpose for you, love, relationships, and parenting. There are thousands of great books, Web sites, and other resources to help you get back on your feet. Here are a few that were helpful to us:

Counseling

- **American Association of Christian Counselors (AACC):** The AACC is a network of Christian counselors and a great place to start looking for the counselor you need. You can find them online at www.aacc.net.

- **Your local church**: Your church will hopefully have a women's ministry or counseling service outreach you can make use of. If nothing else, ask your pastor for some counseling or just a listening ear.

- **Your preferred medical provider**: Family practitioners often have lists of counselors they can refer you to. If nothing else, make sure you're visiting your doctor regularly so he or she can be aware of how you are not just physically but mentally and emotionally.

Support Groups

- **Before You Divorce**: A marriage crisis counseling tool to help you make the right choices before it's too late. Look for them at www.beforeyoudivorce.org.

- **Caring Resources**: Another general grief support group that offers an intensive three-day workshop on grief. More information can be found at www.caringresources.com.

- **DivorceCare**: This is a divorce recovery group with chapters and meetings in churches all across the country. Look for them at www.divorcecare.org.

- **DivorceCare for Kids**: The complementary group designed especially for kids. They're found at www.dc4k.org.

- **Grief Share**: Grief Share is a general grief recovery group that offers help for anyone who's lost someone, regardless of the situation. They're online at www.griefshare.org.

- **New Life Ministries**: New Life is the nation's largest faith-based broadcast, counseling, and treatment organization. You can find tons of information on specific topics at www.newlife.com.

Coparenting

- **Christian CoParenting**: A faith-based group that offers help to blended or split families. Search for them at www.christiancoparenting.com.
- **Stepfamily Survival Guide**: A site that offers support to stepfamilies. It can be found at www.stepfamilysurvivalguide.com.

Finances

- **Dave Ramsey**: Dave is a well-known author, financial advisor, and Christian who provides information and tools on a broad range of financial topics. Look for him at www.daveramsey.com.
- **Crown Financial Ministries**: A faith-based financial-help group, founded by Larry Burkett, that also provides a broad range of advice and tools. They are found at www.crown.org.

Books

Divorce/Grief/Recovery

- Allender, Dan B., PhD. *The Healing Path*. Colorado Springs, Colo.: WaterBrook Publishers, 2000.

- Briscoe, Jill. *Faith Enough to Finish*. Wheaton, Ill.: Tyndale House Publishers, 2001.
- Clinton, Tim, ed. *The Soul Care Bible*. Nashville, Tenn.: Nelson Bibles, 2001.
- Dobson, Dr. James. *Love Must Be Tough*. Sisters, Ore.: Multnomah Publishers, 2004.
- Evans, David G. *Healed Without Scars*. New Kensington, Pa.: Whitaker House, 2004.
- Gillespie, Natalie Nichols. *The Stepfamily Survival Guide*. Grand Rapids, Mich.: Revell Publishers, 2004.
- James, John W., and Russell Friedman. *The Grief Recovery Handbook*. New York: Perennial Currents, 1998.
- Johnson, Nicole. *Keeping a Princess Heart in a Not-So-Fairytale World*. Nashville, Tenn.: Thomas Nelson Publishers, 2004.
- Lucado, Max. *Grace for the Moment*. Nashville, Tenn.: J. Countryman, 2000.
- Naylor, Sharon. *The Unofficial Guide to Divorce*. New York: Wiley Publishing, Inc., 1998.
- Omartian, Stormie. *The Power of a Praying Woman*. Eugene, Ore.: Harvest House Publishers, 2002.
- Petherbridge, Laura. *When Your Marriage Dies*. Colorado Springs, Colo.: Life Journey, 2005.
- Seamands, David A. *Healing for Damaged Emotions*. Colorado Springs, Colo.: Chariot Victor Publishing, 1981.
- Troccoli, Kathy. *Am I Not Still God*. Nashville, Tenn.: W Publishing Group, 2002.

- Ventura, John and Mary Reed. *Divorce for Dummies*. Indianapolis, Ind.: Wiley Publishers, Inc., 1998.
- Wright, H. Norman, and Gary J. Oliver. *A Woman's Forbidden Emotion*. Ventura, Calif.: Regal Books, 2005.

Finances

- Ramsey, Dave. *The Total Money Makeover*. Nashville, Tenn.: Nelson Books, 2003.
- Woodhouse, Violet, CFP, and Dale Fetherling. *Divorce and Money*. Berkeley, Calif.: NOLO, 2002.

Careers

- Bolles, Richard Nelson. *What Color Is Your Parachute? 2005 Edition*. Berkeley, Calif.: Ten Speed Press, 2004.
- Miller, Dan. *48 Days to the Work You Love*. Nashville, Tenn.: Broadman & Holman, 2005.

Audiovisual Materials

- Various. *The Mercy Project*. Nashville, Tenn.: Word Entertainment, 2000.
- Wetzell, Connie. The Healing Word of God Series. Nashville, Tenn.: Nelson Bibles, 2002. www.conniewetzell.com.
- Life After Divorce: This 12-part "Fresh Start Recovery" video series is a wonderful resource for personal guidance and small groups. www.aacc.net.

Notes

1. John Ventura and Mary Reed, *Divorce for Dummies* (Indianapolis, Ind.: Wiley Publishing, Inc., 1998).

2. Elisabeth Kubler-Ross, MD, *On Death and Dying* (New York: Touchstone, 1997).

3. Sharon Naylor, *The Unofficial Guide to Divorce* (New York: Wiley Publishing, Inc., 1998).

4. Dr. Richard Land, *Real Homeland Security* (Nashville, Tenn.: Broadman & Holman, 2004), 99.

5. Elisabeth Elliot in *NIV Woman's Devotional Bible* (Grand Rapids, Mich.: Zondervan, 1990), 721.

6. "Laughter: The New Aerobics?" *Health*, June 2005, 96.

7. Sharon Naylor, *The Unofficial Guide to Divorce*.

Personal Acknowledgments

Grateful thanks to Chip MacGregor, our agent and now our associate publisher. Thanks to Dr. Tim Clinton for his wonderful organization, American Association of Christian Counselors, and for writing the foreword to this life-changing book. Thanks to Peter Robbins for his great photography. Thanks to Ellen Matkowski, Stacie Coe, Fred Wilhelms, Natalie Gillespie, Robert Castillo, Lori Quinn, Jana Burson, and all of our friends at Time Warner, and especially whoever handles our PR and marketing!

Michelle

Where do I begin? First I would like to thank The Conz—the "Italian Stallion" (no joke!)—for listening to my heart and capturing the vision for this book so quickly. And of course, thanks to my other coauthors, Carla and Roz!

I would not be here writing this book if it were not for my mother and best friend, Sandy Hormillosa, who never stopped believing in me when I was at one of the lowest points in my life. And to my father, Tony Hormillosa, who brought healing to me when he walked me up the aisle at church to be prayed for and sat with me to let me know he was there when I needed him most.

Thank you to Shalene Kelly, who walked with me through my marriage, separation, and divorce and listened to me spill my guts. I don't know how you had the patience, but thank you. Thank you to my dear friend, Tammy Maltby, who prophesied over me that "God is going to use this for His glory" and who called me when I was in a moment of despair to speak words of encouragement.

Wes Harbour, what can I say? You are a tremendous counselor. Thank you for helping me forgive and get past my pain. Your prayers, your counsel, are the reasons I Live, Laugh and Love Again.

Marcus, thank you for being a truly great friend. Your heart to care for people and their needs is a beautiful thing.

To my children—Joshua, Aaron, Madison, and Jacob—Mommy loves you. I am so sorry for the pain you have had to endure, the mistakes I made when I was a wreck, the nights I didn't cook dinner, and mornings I didn't get you to school on time. The four of you were the best reasons to press on. You are my joy, and I am thankful for the light you bring to my life.

To my wonderful Lord and Savior Jesus Christ: Without You there would be no book. You pursued me until I was convinced You were there. You held me up when I could not even lift my head. But most of all You have loved me with an unconditional love, and it is this love that gives me the strength and courage to live, laugh, and love again, and again. Thank You, Lord.

Connie

Thanks to Niki, who should be an attorney. To Daniel, who taught me how to work the five remotes and who defragmented my computer, etc. To Dave, Scott, and Chuck, who gave me insight into financial matters. To my dear sweet girlfriends, the ones who prayed with me, cried with me, held me up, and loved me through it all: Sharon, Evelyn, Vickie, Beth S., Beth M., Marcia, Diana, Jeanne, Cindy, and Claudia. Wendy, thanks for keeping me sane during my move. What would I have done without you? To Rick, Paul, Neal, Rod, Carl, Gene, Danny, and Phil for being godly, giving men and for being there for me when I needed you most. To my precious daughters Amy and Erika, who tried so hard to be there for me when they were dealing with their own pain. And to Larry, who really knows how to put together a fax table and who showed me that it's okay to love again.

Finally, I would like to acknowledge my mom (Ma), who recently went to heaven, and thank her for instilling in me the power of prayer and a strong sense of faith in my Creator, and for always reminding me He is in control and "whatever will be, will be." I want to thank her for her fine example of what it's like to walk in forgiveness daily and not hold a grudge. You are my angel. I miss you.

Rosalind

There are many to whom I give thanks. To my family, especially Dad and Mom, my heroes—I did not tell you everything but you both were there for us and provided all the prayers, love, and hugs we needed. To my blessing from God, my son, Joshua—thanks for loving me, especially those times when I was unlovable. You are the *best!* To all of the people who were there during that particular season of my life—thanks for helping me get through some of the phases of my healing process. Each one of you played an important part in my life during that time. Again, *thank you!* To my friends for life—thanks for pushing me when I wanted to give up, for your listening ears, support, love, and prayers. Each one of you is the greatest. Last but not least, to my church leaders and family—thanks for the sermons from the pulpit that encouraged me when I needed an encouraging message. Thanks for the support and resources that were provided for my son and me.

Carla

Thanks to all my girlfriends and "God Chicks": Melissa, I wouldn't be here without you. To Lori, Lynne, Janice, Janet, Jean, Melanie, Kim, Rhonda, Stormi, and Laura, for listening to me whine and cry, helping me move and sell a horse, and sending me great tapes and books during my time of distress. To Dr. Buddy and Mrs. Lilly for your wise counsel. To both of my pastors, Glenn Weekley and Glenn Denton, for being such godly men. For my children Jordan, Olivia, and Colin: May you never need to read this book. I know that God has a purpose in all of this—if only to draw me nearer to Him. To Mom and my sister Crystal, I love you and thank you for standing by me. I love you all.